Let's Talk with Each Other!

Ulf Lubienetzki · Heidrun Schüler-Lubienetzki

Let's Talk with Each Other!

Psychology of Successful Conversation

 Springer

Ulf Lubienetzki
entwicklung GbR
Hamburg, Germany

Heidrun Schüler-Lubienetzki
entwicklung GbR
Hamburg, Germany

The explanations in this chapter are based on the following study letter: Lubienetzki, U. & Schüler-Lubienetzki, H. (2016). LASS UNS MITEINANDER SPRECHEN. GESPRÄCHSFÜHRUNG. Study letter of the Fresenius University of Applied Sciences online plus GmbH. Idstein: Hochschule Freseniusonline plus GmbH.

ISBN 978-3-662-64307-5   ISBN 978-3-662-64308-2   (eBook)
https://doi.org/10.1007/978-3-662-64308-2

This Springer imprint is published by the registered company Springer-Verlag GmbH, DE part of Springer Nature.
The registered company address is: Heidelberger Platz 3, 14197 Berlin, Germany

Preface

For more than two decades we have been dealing professionally with human communication. Whether as coaches, trainers, consultants or even as managers, for us it has always been about exchanging factual information, communicating personal perceptions and feelings, evaluating something or even someone, or even achieving something together with one or more people. Over time, we have gathered a lot of our own experience in communication and have developed our knowledge in a targeted manner. An important part of our work is passing on our experience and knowledge to other people. In our profession, this is mostly done in the form of seminars and training sessions. The great advantage of seminars and training sessions, be it face to face or online, is that it is possible to specifically address the individual questions and needs of the participants. Therefore, the most important component of our events is always the work on case studies that participants bring with them, as well as the development and testing of solutions. Inevitably, the possibilities of reaching people with seminars on communication topics are limited. The cooperation with various universities as well as with Springer Verlag offers us the opportunity to reach significantly more people. We were and are aware that it is in the nature of publications not to be able to respond directly to individual questions and examples from readers. We have therefore taken it as our essential task to convey the knowledge we have compiled on various communication topics as clearly and as closely as possible to what is possible in seminars and training sessions. Three essential elements shape our textbooks for this purpose:

- An engaging and pleasant to read writing style: Textbooks impart knowledge. Putting this knowledge into words in such a way that readers enjoy it was our first goal.
- Vividly developed case studies: The core of the knowledge to be conveyed is to the point in the textbook. Our case studies, which often make you smile or even laugh, direct the focus by translating abstract knowledge into comprehensible action in everyday situations.
- Immediate reflection on what has been learned: Communication is an everyday thing. This means that communication is basically accessible to everyone at all times. In the course of reading our textbooks, we specifically encourage readers to experience and try out what they have just read in their own environment.

We hope you'll find our book both interesting and beneficial.

Ulf Lubienetzki
Hamburg, Germany

Heidrun Schüler-Lubienetzki
Hamburg, Germany
May 2020

Contents

About the Authors

Ulf Lubienetzki

has been working for several years as a consultant, business coach, and trainer with professionals and executives in various industries. In addition, he has more than 20 years of experience as a manager up to the executive level in various national and international management consulting firms. Ulf Lubienetzki holds a degree in engineering and studied social pedagogy and sociology. In the guidebooks and textbooks he has authored, he brings his wide-ranging practical experience from working with his clients to bear.

Heidrun Schüler-Lubienetzki

has been working as a business coach, leadership trainer, management consultant ‚and facilitator for more than two decades. Heidrun Schüler-Lubienetzki is a psychologist with a focus on personnel and organizational development as well as a talk therapist. In more than two decades she has worked with several thousand specialists and executives up to board level. As an author of guidebooks and textbooks as well as specialist, she passes on her knowledge and experience.

Both authors lead together the company entwicklung GbR in their coaching house in Hamburg-Rahlstedt. entwicklung GbR stands for

- Coaching of specialists and managers
- Individual and team training
- Consulting for change processes in organizations

Together with its clients, entwicklung GbR works to maintain and increase the personal performance of specialists and managers, to develop high-performing and efficient teams, to reduce the waste of resources caused by dysfunctional conflicts, and to provide competent advice and goal-oriented support for change.

If you have any questions or need information about personal coaching, seminars, or training, you will find a wide range of information at ► http://www.entwicklung-hamburg.de.

If you have any questions, feedback, or suggestions, please do not hesitate to contact us by e-mail: ► info@entwicklung-hamburg.de.

1

Introduction

The explanations in this chapter are based on the following
study letter: Lubienetzki, U. & Schüler-Lubienetzki, H. (2016).
LET'S TALK. CONVERSATION MANAGEMENT. Study letter of the
Fresenius University of Applied Sciences online plus
GmbH. Idstein: Hochschule Fresenius online plus GmbH.

1

When people meet, they communicate. We can try many things, but we will never manage to avoid communication with another person. So let us submit to the inevitable and think about how we can make communication beneficial and purposeful ...

Communication should enrich our own lives and the lives of others and help us to achieve our goals together. This is true in all areas of life. In the context of this book, we focus primarily on communication in a professional context. Of course, the principles of communication also apply in other life situations. Please do not be afraid to keep them in mind in your private interactions as well.

Even in times of WhatsApp, Facebook and other services, the personal conversation is still the most important form of human communication. That is why we will devote ourselves in this book to the conduct of conversation and deal with the personal attitude as well as the resulting behaviour. In doing so, we will discover that there is more to a conversation than the spoken word. The whole person talks to other people – not only with words, but also with their body language. This realisation has such far-reaching consequences that if there is a lack of coherence between the spoken word and the behaviour displayed, the spoken word becomes distorted in its meaning or even completely incomprehensible.

Comprehensibility is the basic prerequisite for the success of a conversation. However, there are other elements that contribute to the success of a conversation. In this context, we will see how we establish and maintain contact with our conversation partner. We will learn that we ourselves can do a lot to make other people become interested in talking to us. Finally, we will also have a look at situations in which a conversation does not go well and what options we have to improve such situations.

We would like to take this opportunity to share with you, how pleased we are that you are exploring the topics of communication and presentation. Our joy results from the fact that we are absolutely certain that the contents of this book on how to conduct conversations – regardless of your further professional and private goals – will be enriching for you. Awareness of how communication and conversations work will open up opportunities for you to observe what is happening and draw conclusions from your observations in any situation in life. And not only that – you can consciously intervene in what is happening and so actively shape your own experience as well as that of others.

It could start as early as Sunday morning at the bakery. You could order four rolls apathetically, preoccupied with yourself, and the baker hands you back what you want with a professional smile. Goal accomplished, nothing more, nothing less. With your knowledge of communication, you could try something else: You could consciously look at the baker next Sunday and smile kindly at him while saying something friendly. Then ask him for the four rolls. The baker will probably smile back in a friendly way, hand you the rolls, and wish you a nice day or something else friendly. In this case, too, you have achieved your goal and received the four buns. In addition, however, you have given the baker a good feeling and not only that: you also go home not only with the four buns, but also with a good feel-

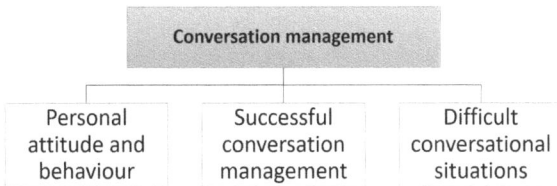

□ Fig. 1.1   The book at a glance

ing. With simple means you have simultaneously bought buns on the subject level and created a good feeling in two people on the relationship level.

A straightforward and everyday situation was designed with simple means. In this book, you will have the opportunity to sharpen and expand your communicative tools for many other situations. The ▣ Fig. 1.1 shows you the structure of this book at a glance.

We will address three central aspects of conducting conversations in this book: the influence of your attitude and behaviour in the conversation on conducting the conversation (▶ Chap. 2), aspects and techniques of successful conducting conversations (▶ Chap. 3) and finally dealing with difficulties and resistance in conversation situations (▶ Chap. 4).

Personal Attitude and Behaviour in Conversation

As the Question, so the Answer

Contents

The explanations in this chapter are based on the following study letter: Lubienetzki, U. & Schüler-Lubienetzki, H. (2016). LASS UNS MITEINANDER SPRECHEN: GESPRÄCHSFÜHRUNG. Study letter of the Fresenius University of Applied Sciences online plus GmbH (Studienbrief der Hochschule Fresenius online plus GmbH). Idstein: Hochschule Fresenius online plus GmbH.

© Springer-Verlag GmbH Germany, part of Springer Nature 2022
U. Lubienetzki, H. Schüler-Lubienetzki, *Let's Talk with Each Other!*,
https://doi.org/10.1007/978-3-662-64308-2_2

2

Do you remember a really good conversation? What was it like? Our guess is that, first of all, the topic was interesting to you and that the conversation got you somewhere personally. But that was not all. Didn't you personally feel very comfortable, somehow just right and valued? And didn't you bring that feeling, that personal attitude, to the person you were talking to, so that they felt comfortable and valued, too? How nice it would be if every conversation were like that. In this chapter, let us take a closer look at what we consider to be the most important building block of a good conversation: the personal attitude of the conversation partner.

🎓 **After Reading This Chapter in Depth, You Will Be Able to …**

- reproduce the **extended communication model** according to Watzlawick et al. as well as the interpersonal circuit diagram and highlight their significance for the personal attitude of interlocutors.
- assess the **relationship** between two communicating parties in terms of symmetry or complementarity.
- classify human **views of life** and **personalities** according to the Riemann-Thomann model and explain their influence on communication.
- differentiate between different **modalities** of communication.
- explain the importance of **congruence** in conversation.

2.1 Basics of the Personal Attitude

We assume that a **conversation** is goal-oriented. Our life experience tells us that there can be other occasions for conversing, but this book is exclusively about conversations that have a specific goal. For example, our goal may be to solve a problem together with our conversational partner or to learn something that will help us personally. The reasons for conversing are endless. Our consistent question should be: How do we achieve our goal in conversations or what leads to success in conversations?

Let us start with the *five axioms of human communication* by Watzlawick et al. (1968) already discussed in the book "How we talk to each other – the messages we send with our words and body language" (Lubienetzki & Schüler-Lubienetzki, 2021). These state that …

1. we cannot not communicate,
2. we communicate on a content and relationship level,
3. we communicate in a circular fashion,
4. we communicate in different modalities (language, behaviour),
5. our communication depends on our definition of a relationship (symmetrical or complementary).

A conversation always involves at least two people or as Schulz von Thun put it (2013, p. 92) Communication is an interaction business with at least two partici-

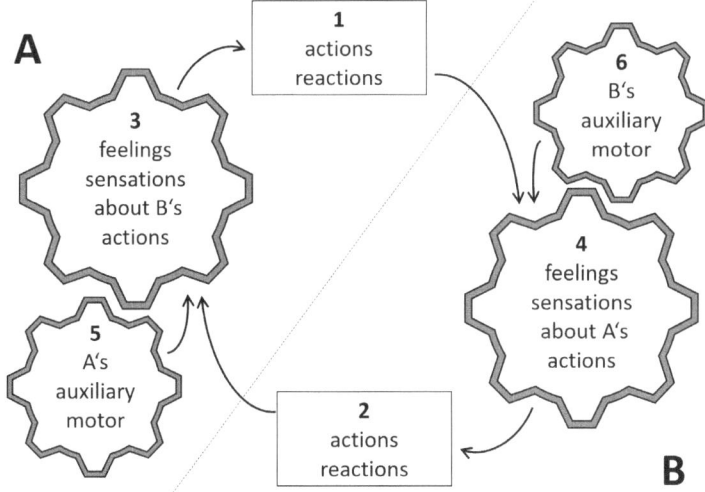

☐ Fig. 2.1 Interpersonal circuit diagram ("vicious circle"). The figure shows a cycle of communication between two people A and B. Statements made by an interlocutor (actions/reactions) activate feelings and sensations in the other interlocutor, who in turn responds with actions and reactions, thereby triggering feelings and sensations in person A. (Source: own representation based on Thomann & Schulz von Thun, 2005, p. 327)

pants. They communicate digitally via language and analogically via their behaviour. The language transmits the content and the behaviour transmits particular messages about the relationship between each other. While conversing, the participants in the conversation influence each other's reactions. In other words, our own behaviour is at least as important for the success of the conversation as the behaviour of our conversational partner. In this context, the conversation partners' view of the relationship is of particular importance (Schulz von Thun, 2013; Watzlawick et al., 1968).

Since our behaviour is so important for the course of the conversation, we want to take a closer look at what our behaviour depends on. The interpersonal *circuit diagram* according to Thomann and Schulz von Thun (2005) can help us here (see ☐ Fig. 2.1, see also Lubienetzki & Schüler-Lubienetzki, 2021).

In the scheme, a distinction is made between external and internal experience. For us, the **external experience** is nothing more than the perceived behaviour (actions, reactions) of our interlocutor. The **inner experience** is what we experience emotionally and what we consciously think about. On the one hand, it influences how we perceive the behaviour of our counterpart and, on the other hand, how we ourselves behave (Thomann & Schulz von Thun, 2005).

Triandis (1971), referring to Rosenberg and Hovland (1960), defines the concept of **attitude**, which is synonymous with **personal attitude**, in this context as follows:

2

Definition ───────────────────────────────────

"an attitude is an idea charged with emotion which predisposes a class of actions to a particular class of social situations." (Triandis, 1971, p. 2)

In other words, our personal attitude or mindset influences our inner experience and also our behaviour.

Case Study

If there is one thing Ms Miller does not like it is writing meeting minutes. As secretary to the owner and managing director of Construction Machines Smith Ltd, she has a pretty good overview of the company, but she does not understand in detail how the technology of their products works and what the production processes are. Therefore, she usually feels insecure and anxious in meetings on these topics, as she fears overhearing something important or misunderstanding and misrepresenting something.

Managing Director John Smith is in a good mood this morning and comes into the office beaming with joy. He greets Ms Miller in a friendly manner and reminds her of the meeting on a new product at 10 a.m., where he needs her to take the minutes. Ms Miller forces a smile and wishes him a good morning as well. John Smith goes into his office. As he does so, he feels irritated and not in as good a mood as he was a few minutes before.

Let us apply the definition of personal attitude to a situational conversation. The conversation involves at least two people who are in a relationship with each other. The conversation is about a factual content, i.e. a topic of conversation. According to Triandis' definition, the personal attitude refers to the social situation. In the example, the topic of conversation and the anxiety it triggered in Ms Miller led to Ms Miller's own behaviour and subsequently to Mr Smith's feelings being influenced. Mr Smith was obviously unable to distinguish what the behaviour shown by Ms Miller referred to.

❓ Reflection Task: Your Childhood Best Friend and Your Personal Attitude

Let us deepen what we have just experienced and start a self-experiment. Please think back to your childhood and to your best friend at that time. Remember the good times and the exciting adventures you had together. Also, remember the warm and comforting feeling of being together. Recall as much as you can. – Have you brought the image and feeling into the here and now? If so, then you can move on. Now imagine that you will soon be working on a project or in a working group with colleagues. You read the list of team members and you cannot believe your eyes, your childhood best friend is also on the list. What is your feeling? What is your attitude towards the upcoming work in the project or work group?

Considering the previous example of Ms Miller and Mr Smith, please answer the following questions:

1. How do you expect the collaboration process will go?
2. How will you behave and how will you communicate with each other?

Try this exercise with a different feeling. What changes when you think back to the worst class bully of your school days and now, surprisingly, you will have to work with him?

In the reflection task, you have actually re-encountered the person from your past who triggered the described feelings in you at that time. Your present personal attitude towards a person can also be influenced by a **transference.**

Definition

Transference is, according to Teuber (2016), a central concept of psychoanalytic theory and practice. In transference, intense unconscious feelings, desires, sensations, or behavioural patterns from important past relationships (...) are actualised in present relationships (...).

In other words, you meet a person whom you do not know, about whom you know nothing and with whom you have had neither good nor bad experiences so far, and yet you spontaneously develop a personal attitude towards this person by transference. If this attitude is negative, for example, because the person reminds you of an unpleasant person from the past, your behaviour may be negatively influenced accordingly. Therefore the relationship building with the person who is actually unknown to you becomes more difficult.

In the next section, we take a closer look at the relationship between personal attitude and behaviour.

2.2 Personal Attitude: Further Approaches

Your personal attitude in the conversation influences your behaviour, your behaviour influences your conversational partner and hence the overall course of the conversation is influenced. Let us apply one of the communication models described in the book "How we talk to each other – the messages we send with our words and body language" (Lubienetzki & Schüler-Lubienetzki, 2021) to this. The **extended communication model** based on Watzlawick et al. (1968) (see ◘ Fig. 2.2).

Two interlocutors are in a relationship with each other and interact. One interlocutor (sender) expresses their opinion on the topic of conversation and behaves, whereupon the other interlocutor (receiver) expresses their opinion and behaves in turn. The conversation itself takes place in an environment or context (e.g. in the office, on the street, etc.).

2

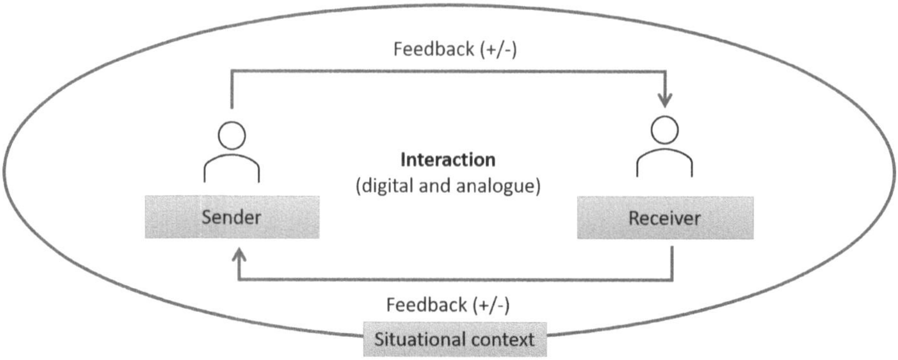

◘ Fig. 2.2 Extended communication model, based on Watzlawick's axioms. The feedback illustrates how much one's own behaviour, which is influenced by one's personal attitude, has an impact on the interlocutor. (Source: own representation based on Watzlawick et al., 1968)

We have already discussed the topic of conversation and our personal attitude towards it. Ms Miller felt insecure and anxious regarding meeting minutes. Her personal attitude then caused her to act accordingly. Her unexpected behaviour made him feel irritated. Whenever a topic of conversation evokes emotions in us, this will also be expressed in our behaviour. Since our conversational partner cannot distinguish between what our emotion and our behaviour refer to without the appropriate background knowledge, it can be helpful to explain our attitudes and thus our behaviours to them. In this way, we avoid our interlocutor attributing our behaviour to themselves or to our relationship with each other.

The same is true for the conversational environment, which can also determine our attitude. For example, think of people who are talking in the subway. You can often observe two types of behaviour. One conversational partner has a much higher proportion of speech, speaks quite loudly and seems to have forgotten their environment. The other is more reserved, speaks more quietly and in short sentences. What personal attitudes do the two of them probably have in relation to the public environment on the train? In this situation, too, one of the interlocutors could refer to the other's reserved behaviour. A short explanation that the other person does not like to discuss private matters in public could help to clarify the situation.

What could we do when our personal attitude towards ourselves, our interlocutor or our relationship with each other is decisive for our behaviour? In this case, we often cannot bring a resolving statement. However, we can make the connections clear to ourselves in order to work on our personal attitude through this insight. In this context, please also think of the transference mentioned in the previous section.

Using Watzlawick et al.'s (1968) fifth axiom, Harris's (1969) views of human life, and an additional view on human personality, we will further approach personal attitudes in the human and interpersonal spheres below.

2.2.1 Relationship Definition Based on Equality (Symmetry) or Inequality (Complementarity)

According to Watzlawick et al. and also Schulz von Thun, our behaviour expresses something about our relationship with our interlocutor. Depending on how we define our relationship, we will consequently behave differently. A fundamental dimension of the definition of relationship and thus of our personal attitude is the relationship between the interlocutors, which can be based on equality (symmetry) or inequality (complementarity) (Schulz von Thun, 2013; Watzlawick et al., 1968). In other words, if we define a relationship as **symmetrical,** we are communicating "on the same level". If we define it as **complementary**, we communicate either from "top down" or from "bottom up". Complementary relationships can be, for example, parent-child relationships, a relationship between teachers and students, or in Star Wars, the relationship between Jedi Knight and Padawan.

> **Important**
>
> We have come across examples of complementary relationships repeatedly in our experience. Of course, the mentioned relationships can also be defined symmetrically by the partners (in the case of the Jedi Knight-Padawan relationship, we are not absolutely sure about this). What is important, however, is that it is about the deeply anchored personal attitude. A relationship does not become symmetrical merely because, for example, a professor allows their students to address him/her by the first name and postulates "We are all equal now!", but at the same time takes over the leadership of a joint working group as a matter of course.

Relationships are also defined in the professional context. Already the professional roles of the interlocutors are provided with expectations. We have often experienced that communication in professional contexts is very successful as long as the expectations of each individual for the respective professional role are fulfilled. If the role expectations differ, communication also falters. Especially between managers and employees, this can become a defining issue. If the mutual expectations are not clarified, different personal attitudes collide, hindering successful communication or even making it impossible. Let us take a look at an example from the company Construction Machines Smith Ltd:

Case Study

Frank Wilson defines his relationship with the trainees as complementary. Translated into his personal attitude, this means that he feels superior to the trainees. He has the idea that trainees should behave respectfully and reservedly towards him. At the same time, he behaves in a deliberately directive and distanced way towards the trainees.

His behaviour causes the trainees to approach him very cautiously. They think twice before approaching him. They usually feel uneasy in his presence.

2

Only one trainee behaves differently. His personal attitude is that all people are equal. He makes a point of speaking to him as an equal. He feels equal to Mr Wilson and acts accordingly in a self-confident manner. This is why there are regular arguments between Frank Wilson and this trainee.

2.2.2 People's Views of Life ("I am okay, you are okay")

Our **views of life** also have a great influence on how we see ourselves and encounter other people. Our personal attitude refers to whether or to what extent we accept ourselves and approach others with appreciation. This is about the person themselves. If I value myself as a person, I can interact with others without fear and with confidence. If I also value my counterpart, I signal to this person through my behaviour that I accept them without reservation. On this basis, factual communication is very successful. Even controversial topics can be clarified objectively and without personal hostility or can be simply left in the room (Harris, 1969).

The situation is different when an interlocutor does not treat themselves and/or the other person with appreciation. A devaluation that is expressed in behaviour, in one or both directions, inevitably leads to the fact that it is no longer about the matter but about the person(s). Therefore, conflict is very likely when two people meet who value themselves but not the other. Unreflectively and without intervention from the outside, such an encounter can escalate quickly, as experience has shown.

Case Study

John Smith attaches great importance to dealing with other people in an appreciative manner. The other day, he met with Andrea Stark, the managing director of a client company. From the first moment, John Smith felt uncomfortable. "What is this all about?" he asked himself. Behaving in a friendly and appreciative manner, as he was accustomed to behaving, it became increasingly difficult as the conversation progressed. Finally, he was glad when the conversation was over. He did not even care in the end whether his product was bought or not. He just wanted to leave. What had happened?

Let us take a look at how the CEO of the client company acted. Personal power is very important to Andrea Stark. She is the boss - she wants to feel that and let others feel it. Mr Smith came just in time for her. "Another one trying to talk me into his product," she thought. So she casually offered Mr Smith a seat and listened to his product presentation with a decidedly bored expression. At the end, she said in an arrogant tone of voice and with a cold smile: "That does not sound bad at all. But I hear about products like this every day, and at much lower prices. Do you not have more to offer?". When John Smith began to reply about the quality of the product she interrupted him harshly: "That is typical for such small companies like yours. You depend on every order and try to persuade people to buy with rambling statements." John Smith ended the conversation politely after this sentence from Andrea Stark and left.

John Smith obviously values himself and others. If he did not value himself, the conversation could have led to the so called **drama triangle** (Gührs & Nowak, 2014, p. 119) described in more detail in the book "How we talk to each other – the messages we send with our words and body language" (Lubienetzki & Schüler-Lubienetzki, 2021). In that case, a person who values themself and devalues others meets a person who does not value themself. Therefore, a devaluing attitude towards others meets a devaluing attitude towards oneself. So the expectations of both persons are confirmed, which has a stabilizing effect. However, the drama is about the parties involved and not around the matter at hand, so that success in a factual topic is not to be expected.

❓ Reflection Task: Drama Triangle with the Wilson Family

We have already covered the following example in the book "How we talk to each other – the messages we send with our words and body language" (Lubienetzki & Schüler-Lubienetzki, 2021). Let's look at the breakfast scene in the Wilson house and answer the following question:

We had already become acquainted with Mr Wilson's basic attitude towards interpersonal relationships in his interaction with the trainees. How would you describe the attitudes of the other participants based on the course of the conversation?

Now for the scene:

Mr Wilson: "Your room looks like a mess again. You never clean up!"

Tommy winces.

Mr Wilson: "I am telling you now for the last time. Clean up!"

Mrs Wilson: "Have you ever taken a closer look at your hobby shed? You cannot put one foot in front of the other there either."

Mr Wilson looks puzzled and remains silent.

Tommy: "Leave it, Dad's right after all."

A little later, Mrs Wilson says to Tommy, "That's the last time I'll be helping you. You always stab me in the back."

Whether Tommy accepts this renewed invitation into the drama triangle remains a mystery. The interaction of the three people involved is interesting: Mr Wilson first invites Tommy into the drama triangle as the persecutor. Tommy takes the bait and moves into the role of the victim. Mrs Wilson comes to her son's rescue as a rescuer.

2

Tommy leaves the victim role and becomes a rescuer himself. Finally, Mrs Wilson, as the persecutor, throws out her bait. If Tommy takes this bait, the drama takes its course again ...

2.2.3 Personality of the Human Being According to the Riemann-Thomann Model

The personal attitude of a person is also closely related to their personality.

Definition

According to the American Psychological Association (n.d.), **personality** is "the enduring configuration of characteristics and behavior that comprises an individual's unique adjustment to life, including major traits, interests, drives, values, self-concept, abilities, and emotional patterns."

The **Riemann-Thomann model** describes the personality in terms of a coordinate system of basic human needs. Closeness and distance (space) as well as constancy and change (time) are in tension with each other (Thomann & Schulz von Thun, 2005) (see ◘ Fig. 2.3).

Closeness and distance in this context are to be understood both physically and emotionally. Thus, a "closeness person" wants to embrace other people, both real and figurative, and to be embraced themselves. A "distance person" prefers to distance themselves and keep other people at a distance both physically and emotionally. A "constancy person" strives for security, that their environment and themselves are reliable and in order. "Change people" strive for the new and surprising, for freedom and adventure. The coordinate system focuses on the temporal dimension in the horizontal and on the spatial dimension in the vertical. If we move along the axes, more and more extreme phenomena arise (Thomann & Schulz von Thun, 2005) (see ◘ Fig. 2.4).

❯ **Important**

There are tensions between the basic needs in the horizontal and vertical axes. We have already dealt with such tension relationships in the book "How we talk to each other – the messages we send with our words and body language" (Lubienetzki & Schüler-Lubienetzki, 2021) in connection with the values and development square (Schulz von Thun, 2008). The further outwards we follow the axes, the more we enter the realm of devaluing exaggerations.

Every personality can be placed in this coordinate system. Depending on the combination of the x-coordinate (closeness-distance) and the y-coordinate (constancy-change), a different personal attitude towards an interlocutor emerges. Imagine a rather distant person who prefers a planned approach meets a rather chaotic person with a strong need for closeness. It is likely that a large part of the conversation

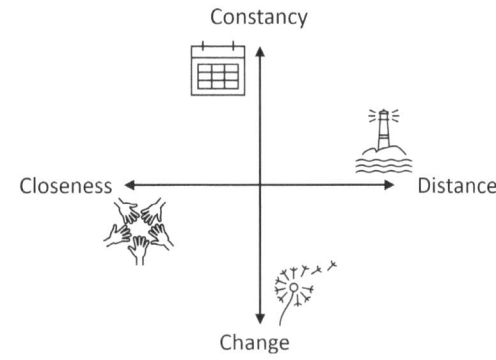

◻ **Fig. 2.3** The four basic needs of the human being. In the Riemann-Thomann model, for describing the human personality, the four basic needs for closeness and distance as well as constancy and change are related to each other. (Source: own representation based on Thomann and Schulz von Thun, 2005, p. 177)

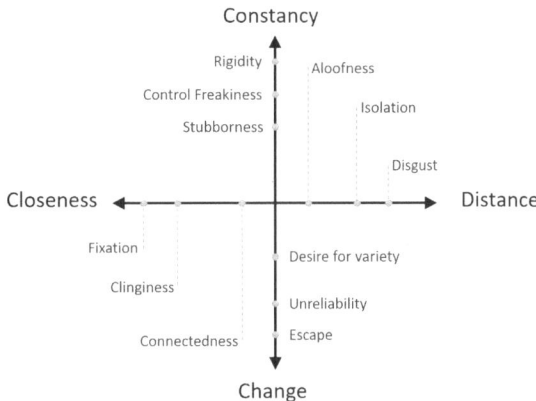

◻ **Fig. 2.4** Expressions of the basic needs. Some examples of personality characteristics along the axes of the Riemann-Thomann model. In principle, any combination along the horizontal and vertical axes is possible. (Source: own representation based on Thomann & Schulz von Thun, 2005, p. 178)

will be determined by how one partner distances themselves and the other follows them in order to achieve physical and emotional closeness. In addition, it will presumably take some time for them to clarify the question of the extent to which deadlines and a planned approach are necessary.

? **Reflection Task: Reflection on Your Own Attitude and Classification of Personality in the Riemann-Thomann Model**

You have learned in the previous sections that, in short, behaviour follows from attitude. Furthermore, you have learned about different ways to think about and characterise a person's personal attitude. Now apply what you have learned to your own communication. Think of a recent conversation that has particularly stuck in your mind. This could have been a particularly pleasant and purposeful conversation or one that went thoroughly wrong and perhaps even ended in an argument.

Use each of the possibilities mentioned and describe your own attitude in the conversation. Which option is best for you to understand? How was your behaviour influenced by your attitude and how did this possibly affect your counterpart?

2

Now look at the Riemann-Thomann model. How would you basically describe your basic needs according to this model and what does this mean for your own sense of well-being? How would you place people close to you, e.g. a dear friend or a person with whom you are constantly in conflict, in this model? How could you better tailor your communication to that person?

2.3   From Attitude Follows Behaviour: The Importance of Non-verbal Communication

According to Watzlawick et al. (1968) human behaviour in the presence of other people is communication, we would even say that the whole human being is communication. If another person perceives us, everything we show of ourselves means something to him. It does not matter whether what we show has something to do with that person or not. In direct conversation, we transmit messages on the analogic channel of our behaviour, which can support what is said, but also turn it into the opposite. We should be aware of this.

> **Important**
>
> In this book, we do not teach you how to tailor your non-verbal communication to achieve specific impressions on your interlocutor. Instead, we refer to the two books by Samy Molcho (a world-renowned mime who has studied body language very intensively). In his books, e.g. "Body Speech" (Molcho, 1985), he deals in words and pictures with different means of effect in facial expressions and gestures. From our point of view, his books contain useful hints to analyse one's own non-verbal communication and to derive specific changes.

According to Watzlawick et al. (1968), human communication has digital and analogic modalities. Language – as a **digital modality** - is particularly well suited for conveying factual content, provided that the interlocutors speak and understand the same language. However, even if we do not understand a foreign language, we can still infer something from listening to or watching someone speaking in a foreign language. Behaviour - the **analogic modality** – communicates to us, for example, a person's emotional state. Of course, what and how much we receive depends on our own "antennae" for receiving emotions. Nevertheless, we will be able to distinguish whether a person is very angry and upset, or whether a person is calm and confident about their subject. Consequently, what works with complete strangers takes on even greater significance in face-to-face conversation. After all, the analogic modality expresses in many ways something about how the relationship with our interlocutor is defined on our part (Watzlawick et al., 1968).

If our attitude, considered in the previous section, takes place within us, our behaviour is directed outward. In other words, everything we show of ourselves in non-verbal ways is perceived and interpreted by others. If another person's interpretation does not match what they expect, irritation and communication breakdowns will occur (Berne, 1966; Schulz von Thun, 2013; Watzlawick et al., 1968).

Watzlawick et al. (1968) stated that the relational aspect in human communication is primarily expressed through the analogic modality, i.e. the behaviour of the person. Combined with the second axiom, which in the first part distinguishes the content and the relationship in communication and in the second part states that the relationship aspect determines the content aspect, it follows that behaviour determines which messages reach our interlocutor.

The first chapter dealt with our personal attitude, which influences the way we conduct conversations and therefore the course of the conversation. We can also assume that our conscious and unconscious behaviour is significantly aligned with our attitude. Therefore, the effect we have on our conversational partner is also determined by our attitude. Successful communication depends not only on what we say, but also, to an overwhelming degree, on how we communicate non-verbally in a conversation. This knowledge is useful to us in two ways: On the one hand, we can observe ourselves, how we feel, what our attitude is towards our conversational partner and how we behave. On the other hand, we can also observe our interlocutor and consciously interpret their non-verbal communication. We can use the information gained in this way to influence the conversation in a goal-oriented way.

> **Important**
>
> Knowledge of non-verbal communication can be used both appreciatively and pejoratively, i.e. with manipulative intent. Our understanding is that the conversations which are the most successful are the ones both conversational partners can unfold free of mutual manipulation. In this context, Schulz von Thun (2013) speaks of a supersummative equation (p. 97) in communication. We also hold this view that in the successful communication between two people, more comes out than the mere sum of what each person brought to the communication. In our view, however, this added value is lost if the participants in the conversation deal with each other with manipulative intent.

The keyword here is *congruence in conversation*. In the book "How we talk to each other – the messages we send with our words and body language", we had already dealt with this concept under the heading "Congruent and incongruent communication" (Lubienetzki & Schüler-Lubienetzki, 2021). According to Schulz von Thun, a congruent message is perceived as consistent in itself. In this case, all verbal and non-verbal signals point in one direction (Schulz von Thun, 2013).

Case Study

Karen Baker describes herself as a bad liar. Her colleagues at Construction Machines Smith Ltd can confirm this. She is just very emotional and cannot hide her emotions well. In customer meetings, however, it is sometimes necessary to promise an appointment even when it is very unlikely that it will be kept. This often goes wrong for Karen Baker. When she makes such promises, she is aware that she is concealing something and has the feeling that she is doing something forbidden, which makes

2

her feel insecure. Her appointment promise is overlaid by her insecurity in these moments.

Some customers do not pay attention to her behaviour or ignore it. However, she has already been asked whether she really believes in her commitment or what a realistic deadline is. Some customers have even interpreted her insecure and reserved behaviour as a personal rejection and have become more reserved in turn.

So our interlocutor receives signals from us and has to interpret them and translate them into messages. In terms of successful communication, we should make this as easy as possible for them. This is often easier said than done. In this context, Schulz von Thun (2013) refers to the sender as having two souls in his chest and an inner muddle (p. 43). The sender feels torn between several messages and the receiver is now faced with a dilemma: They must decide which message to respond to.

For successful communication, this means that incongruent signals should be avoided as far as possible.

Human behaviour has conscious and unconscious parts. We can approach the unconscious parts through feedback and self-awareness (Gührs & Nowak, 2014). In the book "How we talk to each other – the messages we send with our words and body language", we have dealt with this aspect of human communication in connection with the Johari window (Lubienetzki & Schüler-Lubienetzki, 2021).

❓ Reflection Task: Incongruent Communication in Everyday Life

Non-verbal expressions in communication are not necessarily unambiguous. It is often not clear without verbal context whether raised eyebrows are meant to be surprising, questioning or even derogatory. Even a smile can be meant or interpreted in different ways. Now find more examples of how similar non-verbal expressions can have different meanings or be interpreted differently. Afterwards, notice how your facial expressions and gestures could be interpreted in your own behaviour in conversations.

Summary in Key Terms

- A **conversation** takes place purposefully and context-related between at least two parties.
- The **interpersonal circuit diagram** illustrates aspects of the extended communication model according to Watzlawick et al. with regard to the personal attitude of the communicating parties.
  - The circuit diagram differentiates between *external* and *internal* experience.
- The **personal attitude** of a person is expressed in conversation through their behaviour. It can be analysed on the basis of various points of view. These points include, among others, their definition of relationships based on (in)equality,

their outlook on life or their personality, which can be classified in the **Riemann-Thomann model.**

- **Communication** takes place via the *digital* and *analogic* modality, with the latter in particular shaping the relationship between the communicators.
- If a person's modalities prove to be **incongruent**, i.e. contradictory, the communication is disturbed. For successful communication, it therefore makes sense to attach importance to congruent messages.

Literature

American Psychological Association. (n.d.). Personality. In *APA dictionary of psychology*. Retrieved on July 12, 2021, from https://dictionary.apa.org/personality

Berne, E. (1966). *Games people play. The psychology of human relationships*. Deutsch.

Gührs, M., & Nowak, C. (2014). *Das konstruktive Gespräch. Ein Leitfaden für Beratung, Unterricht und Mitarbeiterführung mit Konzepten der Transaktionsanalyse* [The constructive conversation. A guide to coaching, teaching and personnel management involving concepts from transaction analysis] (7th ed.). Christa Limmer.

Harris, T. A. (1969). *I'm OK, you're OK: A practical guide to transactional analysis*. Harper & Row.

Lubienetzki, U., & Schüler-Lubienetzki, H. (2016). *Lass uns miteinander sprechen. Gesprächsführung* [Let's talk to each other. Conversation management] (study letter of the Fresenius University of Applied Sciences online plus GmbH). Hochschule Fresenius online plus GmbH.

Lubienetzki, U., & Schüler-Lubienetzki, H. (2021). *Was wir uns wie sagen und zeigen. Psychologie der menschlichen Kommunikation* [How we talk to each other – the messages we send with our words and body language. Psychology of human communication]. Springer.

Rosenberg, M. J., & Hovland, C. I. (1960). Cognitive, affective and behavioral components of attitudes. In M. J. Rosenberg & C. I. Hovland (Eds.), *Attitude organization and change: An analysis of consistency among attitude components*. Yale University Press.

Schulz von Thun, F. (2008). *Miteinander Reden 2 – Stile, Werte und Persönlichkeitsentwicklung* [Talking to one another 2 – Styles, values and personality development] (32nd ed.). Rowohlt.

Schulz von Thun, F. (2013). *Miteinander Reden 1 – Störungen und Klärungen* [talking to one another 1 – Disturbances and clarifications] (50th ed.). Rowohlt.

Teuber, N. (2016). Übertragung [Transference]. In M. A. Wirtz (Ed.), *DORSCH – Lexikon der Psychologie*. Hans Huber. Retrieved on January 30, 2020, from https://portal.hogrefe.com/dorsch/uebertragung-1/

Thomann, C., & Schulz von Thun, F. (2005). *Klärungshilfe 1 – Handbuch für Therapeuten, Gesprächshelfer und Moderatoren in schwierigen Gesprächen* [Clarification aid 1 – Manual for therapists, conversation helpers and facilitators in difficult conversations] (2nd ed.). Rowohlt.

Triandis, H. C. (1971). *Attitude and attitude change*. Wiley.

Watzlawick, P., Beavin, J. H., & Jackson, D. D. (1968). *Pragmatics of human communication. A study of interactional patterns, pathologies, and paradoxes*. Faber and Faber.

Successful Conversation Management

How Conversations Succeed

Contents

The explanations in this chapter are based on the following study letter: Lubienetzki, U. & Schüler-Lubienetzki, H. (2016). LASS UNS MITEINANDER SPRECHEN. GESPRÄCHSFÜHRUNG. Study letter of the Fresenius University of Applied Sciences online plus GmbH. Idstein: Hochschule Fresenius online plus GmbH.

3

Time is an important factor in today's world. The possibilities to use the available time are almost unlimited. Isn't it desirable to use time wisely then? Certainly, the meaningful use of time means something different to each person. We would like to take a closer look at the portion of personal time in which we talk to other people. We assume that a conversation is fundamentally goal-oriented and consequently we can measure the success of a conversation by whether or to what extent the goal of the conversation was achieved.

🔖 **After Reading This Chapter in Depth, You Will Be Able To …**

- Explain the basics of **value-based conversation** and, on this basis, reproduce the six steps to successful conversation.
- Explain the importance of **situational communication** based on the consistency of situation and person.
- Explain how to **prepare for interview situations** in a structured way by analysing four key aspects.
- Differentiate different **questioning techniques** and forms.
- Apply the concept of nonviolent communication as a **factor that promotes conversation**.

3.1 Basics

So far we have talked about human communication. In this context, Watzlawick et al. and also Schulz von Thun speak of "*metacommunication*" (Schulz von Thun, 2013, p. 101; Watzlawick et al., 1968, p. 40). We will refer to this when we take a closer look at what is probably the most important form of human communication (especially in a professional context): the personal conversation between two or more people.

According to Shannon and Weaver's sender-receiver model (Shannon & Weaver, 1972; cf. also Lubienetzki & Schüler-Lubienetzki, 2021), common language is a necessary condition for conducting conversations. Of course, rudimentary conversations "with hands and feet" are possible; however, we would like to disregard these in this context. Also, there should be no disturbing influences (e.g. noise) in the context of the conversation that distract or prevent mutual hearing and lead to understanding. So much for the more "technical" requirements.

Further insights into human communication (and also our life experience) show that this "technical" view is not sufficient to lead a successful conversation. Mutual understanding does not only result from the fact that one interlocutor says something and the other interlocutor hears what is said. Mutual understanding goes much further and encompasses everything intra- and interpersonal about the interlocutors (cf. also Lubienetzki & Schüler-Lubienetzki, 2021).

Let us look at people whose jobs require them to communicate successfully, such as managers and coaches. These people depend on really understanding the people they work with and being understood by others in the same way. Christiane Hellwig (2016) has summarised the principles that enable managers and coaches, for example, to lead successful conversations under the heading value-based conversation.

> **Important**
>
> We have asked ourselves whether the principles of action contained in the concept of value-based conversation should not apply to all conversations. From our point of view, there is no reason why they should not, so that we extend the concept to any conversation situation.

The approach of **value-based conversation** goes back to the conditions of the therapeutic process formulated by Carl R. Rogers (1959, p. 213). The basic idea of this approach is that therapists help their clients to develop themselves. In doing so, the therapist's support is aimed at the person's tendency or striving for actualization. Rogers defines this **actualizing tendency** as follows:

Definition

The **actualizing tendency** describes a person's striving for the "development toward differentiation of organs and of functions, expansion in terms of growth, expansion of effectiveness through the use of tools, expansion and enhancement through reproduction" (Rogers, 1959, p. 196).

In terms of value-based conversation, we are successful above all by being in the here and now with our conversation partner (and their striving) and by really perceiving and understanding them as a whole. The way we address them and how they understand us depends on our behaviour and therefore on our personal attitude towards them.

In this context, Hellwig (2016) mentions the following **operating principles** of value-based conversation (p. 13), which she derives from the six "Conditions of the Therapeutic Process" (Rogers 1959, p. 213):

1. **Connecting: Getting in touch** – The interlocutors consciously make contact with each other on the relational level. In doing so, they consciously perceive each other. Without contact with each other, the conversation partners remain at a distance and are more with themselves than with the other person.
2. **Incongruence: Sense own incongruity** – One's own attitude should be congruent with the conversation situation. Incongruities have a negative effect on the behaviour and so on the conversation.
3. **Congruence: Finding harmony** – "Feeling, thinking and acting" should match. The whole conversation situation feels right.
4. **Appreciation: Unconditional and positive** – The interlocutors value each other as people. They are honestly interested in each other.

3

5. **Empathy: Experiencing empathy** – Mutual understanding is also achieved emotionally. The outer behaviour and the inner emotional world of the other person should be understood.
6. **Reaching: Feeling resonance** – The climate of the conversation should be coherent for the conversation partners as a whole and without restrictions. They are in the here and now of the topic and really together.

You will have certainly recognised some of the basics of human communication in the above-mentioned principles of action. Following the operating principles formulated by Hellwig, we propose the following six basic steps for successful conversations, whereby a feedback loop to the preceding steps should be established again and again in the course of the conversation (see ◘ Fig. 3.1).

Let's take a closer look at the individual steps and, by means of an example, see what can go wrong if they are not followed:

1. **Establish contact with the interlocutor**

    As banal as this point may sound, we often do not establish real contact with our interlocutors. By contact we mean that we perceive our conversation partner as a whole. In doing so, we are with them and with the matter at hand. If for any reason we cannot be fully with our counterpart, the conversation should be postponed until we can establish real contact. If we cannot choose the time of the conversation, we should actively work on being in the here and now of the conversation. Everything that does not belong to the conversation should be put aside beforehand.

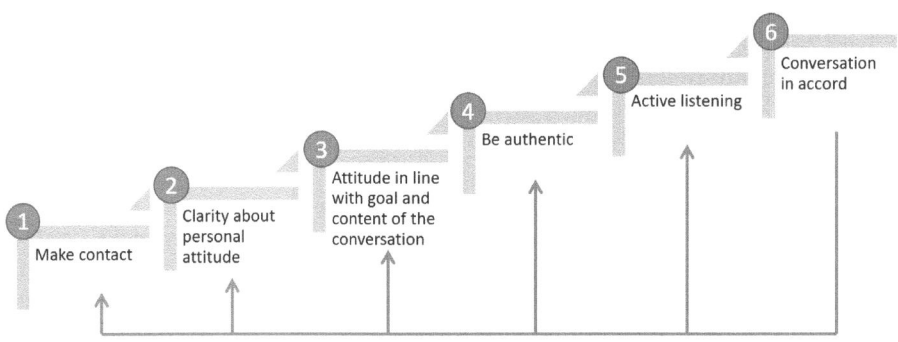

◘ **Fig. 3.1** Six basic steps to a successful conversation. The six steps to a successful conversation are run through again and again in the course of the conversation. They involve questions such as, "Are we still in contact?", "Am I still on-topic and facing the other person?", "Am I myself or am I (unintentionally) playing a role?" or "Do I really want to understand the other person?". An important indicator for readjustment is whether I feel comfortable or not at the moment

Mr Wilson could come any minute now. John Smith wondered why the appraisal interview had to take place today of all days. Once again, all hell broke loose today. He was rushing from one customer appointment to the next. And now, at 6 p.m., Mr Wilson as well. But John Smith wanted to get it over and done with. Mr Wilson was already standing in the doorway. John Smith greeted him curtly and was actually still on his e-mails. "That's just the way it is when you're the boss," he thought. Mr Wilson was sitting across from him, but John Smith wasn't really with him.

2. **Achieving clarity about one's own personal attitude**

Our personal attitude in the conversation determines the conversation (see ► Chap. 2). So we should check this at the beginning of the conversation or, if possible, already beforehand. For a successful conversation, it is absolutely necessary that our attitude is consistent with the content and goal of the conversation (Schulz von Thun, 2013).

John Smith always found Mr Wilson difficult. In his view, he treated the trainees with disdain. On the other hand, he did a good job. The trainees had good grades in their exams, and no one had ever failed. But John Smith did not like this grouchy behaviour from Mr Wilson.

3. **Bringing personal attitude in line with the content and objective of the conversation**

If we send incongruent signals and so messages in a conversation, this behaviour disrupts communication and has an irritating effect on our conversation partner (Schulz von Thun, 2013).

John Smith was actually satisfied with the work results. In the interview he would like to express his satisfaction to Mr Wilson. He would also like to motivate Mr Wilson to behave more appreciatively towards the trainees. Inwardly John Smith was distracted. He was partly on his e-mails and partly looking to keep his distance from Mr Wilson, because secretly he was even a little afraid of hiom. Fortunately, he was the boss.

3

4. **Behave authentically ("genuinely")**

Authenticity creates trust or, the other way round, no one likes to speak to someone who wears a mask. It should be remembered in this context that authenticity has limits where the situation requires adaptation. We will come back to this in the section on situational communication. At this point, we would like to repeat that genuine appreciative behaviour in particular fundamentally supports the success of the conversation.

Case Study

John Smith was inwardly torn. He turned to Mr Wilson and smiled at him. While doing so, he formulated awkwardly that he appreciated Mr Wilson's work with the trainees, but that he wished Mr Wilson would be kinder to the trainees. Mr Wilson listened in silence as his face darkened more and more.

5. **Listen actively (and really fully understand the person you are talking to).**

Active listening and at the same time avoiding everything that leads to communication blocks in our interlocutor. In the book "How we talk to each other – the messages we send with our words and body language" we had already learned about the twelve typical behaviours that lead to communication blocks (Gordon, 1970; Lubienetzki & Schüler-Lubienetzki, 2021).

Case Study

John Smith was taken completely by surprise by Mr Wilson's outburst: "How dare you question my entire work?! Did you have a look at the audit results at all? And anyway", Mr Wilson added, "I would be very curious about your concrete suggestions on how my work could be improved."

6. **Conducting the conversation in mutual harmony (with feedback)**

In mutual harmony means to really feel in the conversation whether the conversation flows. If this feeling threatens to disappear, the previous steps should be questioned again: Are we still in touch? What is my attitude? Am I behaving coherently? Am I authentic? Do I really understand my interlocutor (and do they understand me)?

Case Study

John Smith did not know what to do. After all, he was the boss and could not put up with such behaviour. Actually, he had wanted to praise Mr Wilson and now this. Mr Wilson had apparently got the wrong idea. But what exactly? And what should he do now? So John Smith decided to break off the conversation with the words: "Mr Wilson, you can't talk to me like that. Please calm down first. We will continue our conversation tomorrow." After Mr Wilson had left, John Smith sat at his desk for a long time. How could the conversation have ended like this? And how was it going to continue tomorrow?

? Reflection Task: A Concrete Application of the Six Steps to Successful Conversation

Imagine yourself instead of Mr Smith having to conduct the conversation with Mr Wilson. Alternatively, you can also imagine a similar conversation situation of your own. What would your six concrete steps in the conversation look like in order to achieve the desired successful outcome? Formulate suitable measures and statements for this.

We have first considered the basic steps in an ideal way - with a clear personal attitude and independent of the context or situation in which the conversation takes place. In the next section we will see which role the context or situation plays and how it influences the conversation success in combination with the personal attitude.

3.2 Situational Communication

The personal or inner attitude is, as we have seen in ▶ Chap. 2, of central importance to the conversation. After all, how we behave depends on it. Ideally, it should be absolutely clear and without contradiction, so that what we say and how we behave is consistent. So we should try to bring clarity to our attitude and behaviour. So much for the ideal world. Reality often looks and feels different. Our attitude to a person or to what is brought to us by that person is often not unambiguous and clear. Let's say this person asks us for something as in the following example:

> ▶ **Example: How Should I Act? Different Voices Give Different Answers**
>
> Your neighbour wants to borrow your drill. You do not know each other well and you have never asked him for anything. It comes as surprise then when he comes to your door in the evening and asks you for the drill. How should you act? Here's what might happen inside you in a matter of seconds: Part of you wants to agree immediately; after all, you know from your parents that neighbours should help each other. Another part is not convinced. After all, you wouldn't think of borrowing from a stranger. A third part may be even more suspicious and wonder if you would ever get the drill back. After all, there's the (German) saying, "Never lend something you wouldn't give away." A fourth part of you urges politeness. After all, it would be rude to refuse the request he kindly made.
>
> All these thoughts come to your mind within a breath. The result might be: you force yourself to smile and answer hesitantly, "Of course, uh, gladly. Wait a minute, please, and I'll get it." Or another result: you stare awkwardly into his eyes. Although you own a drill, you say uncertainly, "I'd be happy to lend you a drill. Unfortunately, I don't own

3

one. Why don't you try Ms Brown one floor below?" In both cases, your neighbour probably looks a little irritated, thanks you and says goodbye. ◄

Did you recognise the situation? If so, please don't be surprised - you are not the only one. Schulz von Thun created the image of the so-called **inner team** to describe the inner conflict. Comparable to real team members, members of the inner team take different stances and try to assert their interests. Often it is not possible for a person to identify a clear "winner" and thus a clear attitude. In our example, what is said and what is shown via the behaviour allow different interpretations.. The incongruence within the personal attitude manifests itself in incongruent behaviour on the outside (Schulz von Thun, 2008).

Each person has their own team members who deal with other people and with the situation in which we meet them. Sometimes the constellation fits very well, and the conversation flows. We are clear in attitude and behaviour and feel comfortable in the here and now. These are the best conditions for having a successful conversation. Schulz von Thun (2008) remarks: Ideally, our inner team line-up corresponds to the playing field on which the human encounter takes place. In reality, this correspondence is more or less good (p. 273).

Our conversations take place even when conditions are less than ideal. In these situations, we can only approximate the basic steps of successful conversation mentioned in the previous section. We cannot communicate completely clearly and authentically in such situations, but must adapt our communication to the situation.

► **Example: Situational Communication**

The following annoying statement might also have suited the inner constellation in our example: "Please don't disturb me in the evening. I don't want to lend you my drill. Goodbye." This response might have been very authentic and would have matched our personal attitude perfectly. Also, we would certainly not be bothered by our neighbour again until further notice. In the long run, however, we would probably have destroyed any possibility of social contact with the neighbour. And who knows, we might even need his help 1 day. ◄

The situation is of great importance in determing whether a conversation is successful or not. There are four ways in which our behaviour can match our inner attitude and the situation. The following diagram in ◘ Fig. 3.2 according to Schulz von Thun shows these four options (Schulz von Thun, 2008).

Let's go through the individual fields clockwise using an example:

Case Study

John Smith, as managing director of Construction Machines Smith Ltd, is looking for an assistant. Four applicants are shortlisted. John Smith interviews each person in turn in his office.

The conversation with Ms Right flowed naturally John Smith had a good feeling right from the start and it was the same with Ms Right. Ms Right's entire demeanor matched the occasion of the conversation. She had prepared herself well and

	In accordance with the situation	**Not** in accordance with the situation
In accordance with oneself	**consistent**	**inappropriate**
Not in accordance with oneself	**feigned**	**awry**

🖸 **Fig. 3.2** Four-field scheme for the concept of consistency of behaviour with the person's inner attitude and the situation. There are four ways in which our behaviour can match our inner attitude and the conversation context. (Source: own representation based on Schulz von Thun, 2008, p. 306)

appeared natural and competent. She also had questions for John Smith that showed genuine interest. John Smith looked at his watch after more than an hour and was completely surprised at how quickly the time had passed.

After that came Mr Offside. Mr Offside was at least as competent as Ms Right. He answered all questions absolutely correctly and was even able to add aspects that John Smith himself had not even thought of. Mr Offside also seemed very authentic. Only this meant that Mr Offside always addressed John Smith with his first name and also did not spare any expletives. John Smith was deeply impressed by Mr Offsides' competence, but his open authenticity clearly went too far for a job interview.

Ms Peculiar was the third candidate. She was also very competent and could express herself excellently. She also asked very intelligent questions. After the interview, however, John Smith could not remember exactly how they came to talk about Ms Peculiar's grandmother. It was probably related to the question why Ms Peculiar moved to another place of residence. Ms Peculiar was visibly touched because her grandmother suffered from dementia and had to live in a nursing home. She had tears in her eyes when she told him about it. John Smith did not know how to react. He had known Ms Peculiar for just half an hour and listened to her grandmother's tragic story. Actually, he didn't want to know or talk about it at all; after all, it had nothing to do with the vacant position. Nevertheless, he tried to pull himself together and talked to Ms Peculiar in the hope that she would calm down. After the conversation, John Smith wondered what drove Ms Peculiar to talk about herself and her grandmother in such a way. But he found it even more bizarre that, although he aimed at something else, he got involved with the subject of her grandmother.

Mr Opportune somehow reminded John Smith of Mr Offside. He just couldn't tell why. Mr Opportune was, like the three other applicants, very competent. He was smartly dressed and spoke in a decidedly slow and deliberate manner. In the course

3

of the interview, Mr Opportune frequently moved his shoulders, as if the suit didn't fit properly. Something seemed unusual about him. He was a polished speaker, but at the same time his speech seemed stilted and not very lively. All in all, he gave John Smith the impression of a bad actor. In retrospect, he thought, "Mr Opportune was almost like Mr Offside trying to behave himself."

Based on the examples, we can see that the expectations we have of the people in question derive from the situation. Expectations determine the behaviour that people should show in a certain situation which ideally is consistent with the person's inner attitude (Schulz von Thun, 2008). John Smith has certain expectations of the role of the applicant. If the behaviour deviates, he is irritated and consequently focusses no longer on the competent answers of the applicants.

? ? Reflection Task: Personal Experience with (In)consistencies in a Conversation
Please think of conversation situations where you had the feeling that something was not right. How did you and your counterpart behave and express yourselves? Please classify the conversation situation in the four-field scheme.

3.3 Conversation Preparation

In a professional context, conversations often do not take place spontaneously or by chance, but are planned and scheduled. Examples of such conversations are One-on-One meetings between manager and employee in which different topics can be discussed, including:
1. **information and status updates** – a person or group is informed about an issue such as the progress or next steps in a project.
2. **delegation of tasks** – an employee is given and explained a work assignment.
3. **feedback/criticism** – an employee receives positive or critical feedback on personal work performance or behaviour in the workplace.

We usually have the opportunity to prepare for these meetings. The six basic steps for successful conversations outlined at the beginning of this chapter provide an initial guide for preparation. These steps should be followed in order to prepare for the interview and examined for possible "stumbling blocks".

The interview situation is of particular importance (see ▶ Sect. 3.2). One possibility for structured preparation for the interview situation is the analysis of the **background, thematic structure, interpersonal structure** and **objectives** (Schulz von Thun, 2008). In the following, we would like to use these aspects stated by Schulz von Thun and compile what we consider to be the most important contents of the preparation:

1. **Background**

   This includes everything that has happened beforehand and is relevant to the conversation. The central question is for the cause for the conversation (Schulz von Thun 2008). The background also includes everything that is relevant for the relationship with our interlocutor and our own attitude towards them (Gührs & Nowak, 2014).

2. **Thematic structure**

   The topic should be consistent with the reason for the discussion and the objective. If available, an agenda or list of topics provides clarity. It can also be important to determine what is not part of the topic (Schulz von Thun, 2008). In negotiation situations, it is helpful to gather arguments and counter-arguments in advance. In particular, you should know your negotiation options in case you agree, but also in case you do not agree (Gührs & Nowak, 2014).

3. **Interpersonal structure**

   The people present and the roles they embody are important. It's also important how they relate to one another (Schulz von Thun, 2008).

4. **Objective**

   What is to be achieved in the conversation? Which criteria define its success? One's own goals are important, but at least as important are those of the interlocutor(s). Deviating objectives should be clarified in advance or at the beginning of the conversation (Schulz von Thun, 2008).

   Since, as mentioned, our premises in preparing the conversation do not necessarily have to coincide with those of our counterpart, it has proven useful to explicitly clarify the situation at the beginning of the conversation. A brief summary based on the following question is suggested by Schulz von Thun (2008, p. 285):

» How come [...] and what sense does it make [...] that I of all people [...] want to work with you of all people [...] on this subject [...]?

? Reflection Task: Prepare Your Next Most Important Conversation

There is bound to be an important meeting for you in the near future. Prepare it in a structured way as shown. Is the result fine for you and do you feel well prepared? If yes, then let's go into the conversation. If something is still missing, then please complete the four points accordingly, so that you can come back to them in preparation for the next important conversation.

3.4 Questioning Techniques

In the interpersonal circuit diagram according to Thomann and Schulz von Thun, a distinction is made between external and internal experience in the communication cycle (Lubienetzki & Schüler-Lubienetzki, 2021; Thomann & Schulz von Thun, 2005).

Applied to our goal of having a successful conversation, this means that the better we understand what moves our conversation partner inside, the more likely

3

our statements will be understood by our conversation partner. For this reason, we should really turn towards our interlocutor in the conversation, get into contact with them, and perceive the person as a whole. In this context, perceiving the person means listening to what they say and seeing how they behave.

As you already know, Watzlawick et al. (1968, pp. 60–66) refer to this issue with the terms *digital* and *analogic modalities*. Language is able to verbalise complex relationships through its defined syntax and the semantics of words and concepts. Language has weaknesses when it comes to messages that express feelings and the relationship between people. That, in turn, is a strengths of analogic modality, i.e. behavior, which logical syntax, and might be ambiguous. For example, a smile can express friendship or contempt (Watzlawick et al., 1968).

By listening to our interlocutor and perceiving them as a whole, we learn many things that help us decode their messages and understand the messages behind the message. We learn even more when we **listen actively** rather than passively: "In active listening, the receiver tries to understand what it is that the sender is feeling or what his message means" (Gordon, 1970, p. 53). To achieve this understanding, the receiver has the opportunity to ask questions and paraphrase without judgment what they have understood (Gordon, 1970).

Questions are therefore the most important method for understanding our counterpart in a conversation. But questions can do even more: they can steer a conversation. They can help our counterpart to develop themselves further or to remove blockages, and unfortunately they can also be misused for manipulative purposes (Gührs & Nowak, 2014).

Ruth Cohn, the founder of *Theme-centered interaction*, a concept for working with groups, said: When you ask a question, say why you are asking and what the question means to you. Express yourself and avoid the interview (Cohn, 1980, p. 124). We subscribe to this phrase.

> **Important**
>
> When we deal with questions and questioning techniques, the questions that are particularly important for us are those that are asked in the sense formulated by Ruth Cohn. Successful communication is supported by these questions. Questions can also be asked with a manipulative motive which we will deal with in the following. You should know these questioning techniques and be able to recognise them in order to effectively counter them in your conversation.

Questions can be open or closed.

> **Definition**
>
> A **question** is **open** if it does not contain any restrictive specifications, such as answer options (adapted from Gührs & Nowak, 2014; Friedrichs & Schwinges, 2015).

Mostly open questions are introduced with W-question words, e.g. "who", "what", "where", "when", "why", etc. Open questions have the advantage that the questioner can obtain a lot of information with a short question. However, this can lead to information overload.

Definition

Closed questions specify the answer options (e.g. yes or no). This also includes questions that specify alternatives (adapted from Gührs & Nowak, 2014; Friedrichs & Schwinges, 2015).

Closed questions have the advantage that factual content can be clarified. They have the disadvantage that after the short answer, the ball is back in the questioner's court (Gührs & Nowak, 2014; Friedrichs & Schwinges, 2015).

Open and closed questions can be formulated with different objectives. Often, the aim is not only to obtain factual information, but also to achieve a certain effect with the interviewee and in the conversation by using suitable questioning techniques.

The following list is not exhaustive, but in our view it contains the most important **question types** and **techniques** (cf. Gührs & Nowak, 2014; Friedrichs & Schwinges, 2015):

1. **Information question** ("What do you want to know?")

   The information question is usually designed as an open question. The question serves to gather information. It should be formulated briefly and, as an open question, usually begin with a W-word.

► Example

Karen Baker talks to John Smith about yesterday's customer meeting. John Smith asks: "How did the customer react to the product presentation?" After Karen Baker explained the customer's positive reaction to him, John Smith asks, "That sounds great. Why didn't you come to me yesterday?" Karen Baker falters briefly and replies, slightly embarrassed, "It was already after 5 p.m. and I still had a private appointment." John Smith quickly replies, "That was perfectly fine." ◄

❯ Important

The question word "Why?" should be used with caution, as it asks the respondent to justify themselves. It puts them in a corner. They have to position themselves and "show their colours", which can have a blocking effect. The flow of the conversation can be interrupted and the person being asked "why" closes themself off.

2. **Alternative/decision question** ("Have you decided?")

   Formulated as a closed question, the question in its basic form expects a yes or no answer. In its extension, the respondent is offered alternatives from which they can choose one. The conversation may stall if the respondent does not agree to any of the alternatives. The questioning technique can be used with aggravating or manipulative intent by offering unequal alternatives.

> ► Example

John Smith looks for a customer file and asks Ms Miller: "Ms Miller, do you have the file from the Bolt company?" Ms Miller replies, "No, unfortunately not."

A little later, John Smith asks Ms Miller: "The company party ... where would you prefer to celebrate it? In our atrium, on the sports field or at the Hotel Proud?" Ms Miller answers, "I would like our atrium best." ◄

3. **Counterquestion** ("Why do you even want to know?").

The interlocutor's question is not answered, but they are also asked a question. This procedure can be useful if the interlocutor tries to distract from the actual core of the conversation with questions, or tries to withhold information. Frequent counter-questions hinder the course of the conversation and can even lead to a power struggle.

> ► Example

Mr Wilson asks Ms Baker: "Surely you also think that the trainees need strict guidance?" Ms Baker asks back, "What does Mr Smith think about that?" Mr Wilson looks irritated and asks more openly, "How would you lead the trainees?" ◄

4. **Motivating question** ("Great! What do we want to do next?")

The motivational question contains praise or positive attribution. It is designed to encourage the interlocutor to answer and to come out of their shell. The mood of the conversation should be positively influenced. It is important that the praise is actually expressed with appreciative intent. So, fake praise in a motivational question can be used with manipulative intent.

> ► Example

John Smith asks Mr Wilson, who has been rather reserved in the discussion so far: "Mr Wilson, you as a proven specialist for product A ..., what would you advise our customer?" ◄

5. **Shock/attack/provocation question** ("Do you actually know what you just said?").

The questioner wants to lure the interlocuter from sitting on the fence. They should leave their unclear position and take a clear stance. With manipulative intent, such a question could be used to elicit unintended statements from the interlocutor.

> ► Example

Karen Baker and Mr Wilson once again disagree about the trainees. Mr Wilson talks about the old days and how he was treated as a trainee. Karen Baker suddenly asks him, "Do you really think we can get anywhere with these antiquated methods today?" ◄

6. **Solution-oriented question** ("How would you tackle this?")

The solution-oriented questions aim to support the respondent in finding their own solutions to problems. They are posed in the subjunctive and ask the respondent hypothetically to adopt a different perspective. The other perspective can be that of another person or it can also anticipate a future development.

► **Example**

John Smith has a coach who supports him in difficult business situations. This time it is about the working relationship with Mr Wilson. John Smith has the feeling that he is not reaching Mr Wilson and that he is doing what he wants. His thoughts have been revolving around this problem for some time. The coach wants to support Mr Smith in finding a solution and asks him the so-called miracle question: "Mr Smith, imagine you wake up in the morning and a fairy has worked a miracle. Your problem with Mr Wilson is solved. Since you were asleep, you naturally do not know that the miracle has been worked. Nevertheless, how would you know that the miracle had happened?" ◄

7. **Question with manipulative intent** ("Certainly you already expected this question, right? Who wouldn't?")

The leading **question** pushes the respondent in a desired direction. The true opinion is not interesting, rather the suggested opinion is to be adopted. Suggestive questions often contain words such as "certainly", "obviously", "clearly", "surely" etc. **Rhetorical questions do** not expect an answer. Rather, the answer is already contained in the question. The questioner assumes that the respondent has the same opinion. The **indirect question**, often phrased as a trick question, aims to get an answer to a question that cannot be asked directly. The questioner may also try to disguise their own opinion by addressing a topic only indirectly.

► **Example**

John Smith is negotiating with an unpleasant customer. After they had talked about the advantages of the product for over an hour, the customer asks: "Now you have listed the advantages of your product to me for over an hour. You also know that the same product is 20% cheaper at your competitor, right? Would you pay about 20% more for the same product?" John Smith answers with a counter-question (trying to find out if the customer is just bluffing): "So, according to our competitor, their product has the same features as ours. Then why have we been sitting here together for over an hour?" ◄

❓ **? Reflection Task: Questioning Questions Put to You**

Recall situations in which you were asked questions and in which you asked questions yourself. What type of question was it in each case? What was the likely intention of the question and what intention did you have when asking your question?

3.5   Factors That Promote and Inhibit Dialogue

In this section, we would like to direct our attention to the factors that promote or inhibit successful conversation. In order to systematise the various factors, we will again recall the extended communication model based on Watzlawick et al. (1968) with ◘ Fig. 3.3.

Now we apply this model to a conversation situation in a certain environment (e.g. office, canteen, etc.). We are the sender and the receiver is our conversation partner. We interact with each other; in doing so, we express ourselves verbally and non-verbally.

Let's start with the environment. This can have an influence that promotes or inhibits conversation. Certainly, we cannot always choose the environment in which a conversation takes place. However, if we have the choice, a calm and pleasant conversation environment has a beneficial effect on our conversation.

Of course, we ourselves and our interlocutor are at the centre of the conversation. We have already learned about the following **factors that promote and inhibit conversation:**

1. **Personal attitude**

   The personal attitude can be viewed from different angles. According to the fifth axiom of Watzlawick et al. the relationship can be based on equality or inequality (Watzlawick et al., 1968). Also, the view of life can be taken as a guide. This is either positive or negative, i.e. appreciative or depreciative towards ourselves and others (Harris, 1969). As a third possibility we have looked at the personality of the person. For this purpose, we distinguished the dimensions of closeness and distance (space) as well as constancy and change (time) according to the Riemann-Thomann model (Thomann & Schulz von Thun, 2005). Whether the personal attitude promotes or inhibits conversation depends on both conversation partners. If the personal attitudes match, for example if both interlocutors define their relationship to each other in the same way, this has a conversation-promoting effect. Conversation is inhibited, on the other hand, if,

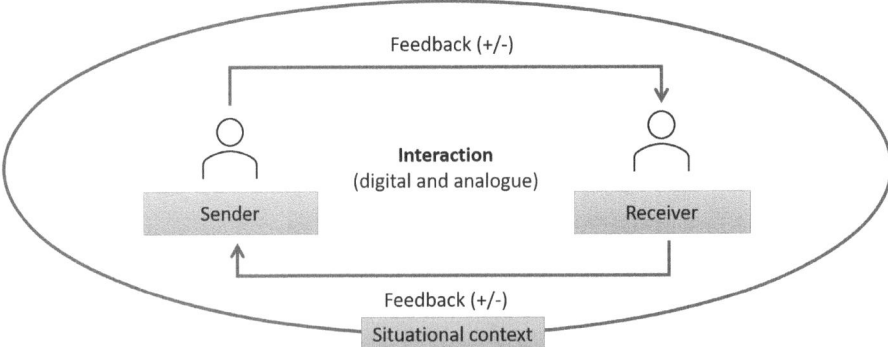

◘ **Fig. 3.3** Extended communication model, based on Watzlawick's axioms. The extended communication model based on the axioms of Watzlawick et al. shows various factors that can promote or inhibit conversation. (Source: own representation based on Watzlawick et al., 1968)

for example, one interlocutor has an appreciative attitude towards themselves and towards others and the other interlocutor responds with devaluation.

2. **Congruence and incongruence**

   If what we say and what we express non-verbally does not match, this can have an irritating effect on our conversation partner (Schulz von Thun, 2013). Such irritation can have a conversation-inhibiting effect. Clarity in our attitude as well as authenticity and congruence in our behaviour, on the other hand, have a conversation-promoting effect (Hellwig, 2016).

3. **Behaviour appropriate to the situation**

   If our conversation partner perceives our behaviour as consistent with the conversation situation, this can have a positive effect on the conversation. The authenticity mentioned in the previous point can, if it does not match the situation, have an irritating effect and thus inhibit the conversation. If we have the opportunity, we should prepare ourselves for the conversation situation (Schulz von Thun, 2008).

4. **Communication barriers and active listening**

   The typical 12 communication barriers according to Gordon, for example any kind of judgement or evaluation, have a conversation-inhibiting effect. Active listening, with the aim of understanding the interlocutor in all facets, including their feelings, promotes conversation (Gordon, 1970).

   Another way of communicating in a way that promotes conversation is offered by the **concept of nonviolent communication** according to Marshall B. Rosenberg (2005). At the heart of this concept is the thesis that we really get in contact with people when we are empathetic with each other. Contact in this context means that we are really with the other person - with what they say and with how they feel. As with Gordon (1970), understanding the interlocutor without judgment or moralising is at the heart of nonviolent communication (Rosenberg, 2005).

   Nonviolent communication can be seen as a process consisting of four components (see ◘ Fig. 3.4):

1. **Observing** and really perceiving our counterpart is the first challenge. Most of the time we mix up observations and evaluations when we talk about something. Often we even confuse an observation with an evaluation (Rosenberg, 2005).

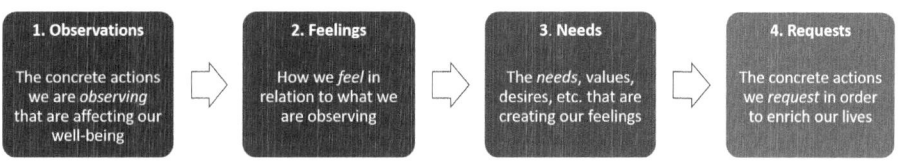

◘ **Fig. 3.4** Process of nonviolent communication according to Rosenberg. According to Rosenberg, the process of nonviolent communication can be divided into four components. (Source: own representation based on Rosenberg, 2005)

3

We had already experienced Mr Wilson dealing with trainees before. For the umpteenth time, Mr Wilson finds a trainee's workstation after hours with various documents and tools scattered about. One of Mr Wilson's training principles is "workplaces are left tidy." Mr Wilson gets annoyed and decides to talk to the trainee in question the next morning. Knowing Mr Wilson so far, we can imagine that the conversation will be rather one-sided and heated. In the end, Mr Wilson and the trainee will be very upset and neither will be sure how to proceed.

You have already learned about the "miracle question". Let's do a thought experiment based on it: Overnight, a fairy godmother appeared to Mr Wilson and taught him the concept of nonviolent communication. How would the trainee experience his conversation with Mr Wilson the next morning?

Mr Wilson first greets the trainee in a friendly manner and tells him in an appreciative attitude that he would like to talk to him about his workplace. He says the following: "Yesterday evening I went past the trainees' workplaces again. I noticed that there were various documents and several tools scattered around your workstation."

So much for Mr Wilson's observation. It was important for him not to include any evaluation in his observation. Sentences such as "Your desk was untidy." or "You only partially tided up." contain an evaluation and would probably have led to the trainee adopting a justification attitude, which would have led to a blockade. ◄

2. Now it is important to explore one's own **feelings** during the observation. Revealing one's feelings allows the interlocutor to gain an understanding of the other person's attitude and behaviour (Rosenberg, 2005).

After Mr Wilson has shared his observation with the trainee, he speaks of the feelings triggered by that: "When I found your desk like that yesterday, I was angry at first. After thinking about it further, I realised that I felt disappointed and hurt."

At this point it was important for Mr Wilson to formulate his feelings in relation to the observation and not to the trainee. Sentences like "You made me angry." or "You are a disappointment." would not have been appropriate for the situation last night - the trainee was not present, after all. Such statements would probably have caused blocking defensive reactions in the latter. ◄

3. The **needs** behind the feelings are to be verbalised in the next step. This constructivist view means that it is not other people who are responsible for our feelings and behaviour, but always ourselves (Rosenberg, 2005).

Once Mr Wilson was aware of his feelings, he also knew where they came from. Deep inside, he has a desire for respect and appreciation. For example, he said, "I was disappointed and hurt because the principle 'workplaces are left tidy' is very important to me. When people don't stick to that principle, it's derogatory in my eyes."

> Mr Wilson relates the need and his reaction to himself and not to the trainee. It was not the trainee as a person who hurt him, but that the principle was not observed. ◄

4. In the last step, a **request** is formulated, the fulfilment of which increases the quality of life of the interlocutors. For this purpose, the request should be formulated positively. We do not ask to stop or not to do something, but rather formulate how something should be done or how we would like it to be (Rosenberg, 2005).

► Example

Finally, Mr Wilson formulated his request, "Please move the documents and tools to your workstation in the compartments provided."

The trainee was visibly surprised. He had known Mr Wilson differently until then. So he answered: "Of course, Mr Wilson, I understand."

In a nonviolent way he could also have answered: "If you see documents and tools lying on a workplace in the evening, then you feel violated. It is important to you that the principle 'workplaces are left tidy' is observed. Of course, I will clean up the workstation immediately and in the future I will observe this principle." ◄

The four components of nonviolent communication according to Rosenberg show that communication is always promoted when people really come into contact with each other and understand what moves others and what their needs are. "Life-alienating communication", as Rosenberg (2005, p. 15) calls it, on the other hand, has a blocking effect. He includes "moralistic judgments" (p. 15), "making comparisons" (p. 18), "denial of responsibility" (p. 19), "make demands" or even "reward" and "punishment" (p. 22).

? Reflection Task: Revisit and Summarise a Past Conversation with Regard to Nonviolent Communication

When recently have you felt the need to really tell another person what you think and have you acted on it with them? Please recall the course of the conversation. What did your counterpart receive and how did it affect them?

Let us assume that the fairy godmother also appears to you and you have the opportunity to conduct the conversation once again along the four components of nonviolent communication. Which words would you choose?

Summary in Key Terms

- Conversations are fundamentally goal-oriented, which means that the **success of a conversation** is measured by the extent to which the pursued **goal of the conversation** was achieved. With the help of certain procedures, the chances of success of the conversation can be influenced.
- In **value-based conversation,** one basically assumes that communication is successful when one consciously perceives and wants to understand one's conversation partner in the here and now.
  - Based on the 6 *operating principles of value-based conversation,* one should therefore in a conversation ...

3

1. Establish contact with the interlocutor
2. Achieve clarity about one's own personal attitude
3. Bring the personal attitude in line with the content and goal of the conversation
4. Behave authentically ("genuinely")
5. Listen actively (and really understanding the other person)
6. Conduct the conversation in mutual harmony (with feedback!)

— The concrete form of the six steps depends on the discussion situation.
— The **personal attitude** and the degree of authenticity of the communicator must be adapted to the **conversation situation.**
  — A person can clarify their inner attitude, among other things, by setting up the **Inner Team** in the sense of Schulz von Thun.
— If possible, one should prepare for an interview, especially in a professional context. **Structured preparation** for the interview can be done by analysing the background, the thematic structure, the interpersonal structure and the objective of the interview.
— In the conversation itself, one's own behaviour should be **conducive to conversation.**
  — Certain **questioning techniques** can be consciously used for this purpose.
  — Active listening, congruent and situation-appropriate behaviour as well as an appreciative attitude towards the conversation partner have a positive effect on the chances of success of the conversation.
  — The *process of nonviolent communication* developed by Rosenberg (2005) offers guidance:
    1. Observe the other person and perceive without judgement
    2. Explore and reveal your own feelings
    3. Express needs behind feelings
    4. Formulate positive requests, the fulfillment of which increases the quality of life of the interlocutors

Literature

Cohn, R. (1980). *Von der psychoanalyse zur themenzentrierten Interaktion. Von der Behandlung einzelner zu einer Pädagogik* [From psychoanalysis to theme-centred interaction. From the treatment of individuals to a pedagogy] (4th ed.). Klett-Cotta.

Friedrichs, J., & Schwinges, U. (2015). *Das journalistische interview* [The journalistic interview] (4th ed.). Springer.

Gordon, T. (1970). *Parent effectiveness training: The no-lose program for raising responsible children.* P. H. Wyden.

Gührs, M., & Nowak C, (2014). *Das konstruktive Gespräch. Ein Leitfaden für Beratung, Unterricht und Mitarbeiterführung mit Konzepten der Transaktionsanalyse* [The constructive conversation. A guide to coaching, teaching and personnel management involving concepts from transaction analysis] (7th ed.). Christa Limmer.

Harris, T. A. (1969). *I'm OK, you're OK: A practical guide to transactional analysis.* Harper & Row.

Hellwig, C. (2016). *Wertebasierte Gesprächsführung – Wirkprinzipien des personenzentrierten Ansatzes* [Value-based conversation - operating principles of the person-centred approach]. Springer.

Lubienetzki, U., & Schüler-Lubienetzki, H. (2016). *Lass uns miteinander sprechen. Gesprächsführung* [Let's talk to each other. Conversation management] (study letter of the Fresenius University of Applied Sciences online plus GmbH). Hochschule Fresenius online plus GmbH.

Lubienetzki, U., & Schüler-Lubienetzki, H. (2021). *Was wir uns wie sagen und zeigen. Psychologie der menschlichen Kommunikation* [How we talk to each other – the messages we send with our words and body language. Psychology of human communication]. Springer.

Rogers, C. (1959). A theory of therapy, personality and interpersonal relationships as developed in the client-centered framework. In S. Koch (Ed.), *Psychology: A study of a science. Vol. 3: Formulations of the person and the social context* (pp. 184–256). McGraw Hill.

Rosenberg, M. B. (2005). *Nonviolent communication. A language of life* (2nd ed.). PuddleDancer Press.

Schulz von Thun, F. (2008). *Miteinander Reden 3 – Das "innere team" und situationsgerechte Kommunikation* [Talking to one another 3 – The "inner team" and situational communication] (17th ed.). Rowohlt.

Schulz von Thun, F. (2013). *Miteinander Reden 1 – Störungen und Klärungen* [Talking to one another 1 – Disturbances and clarifications] (50th ed.). Rowohlt.

Shannon, C. E., & Weaver, W. (1972). *The mathematical theory of communication* (5th ed.). University of Illinois Press.

Thomann, C., & Schulz von Thun, F. (2005). Klärungshilfe 1 – Handbuch für Therapeuten, Gesprächshelfer und Moderatoren in schwierigen Gesprächen [Clarification aid 1 – manual for therapists, conversation helpers and facilitators in difficult conversations] (2nd ed.). Reinbek: Rowohlt.

Watzlawick, P., Beavin, J. H., & Jackson, D. D. (1968). *Pragmatics of human communication. A study of interactional patterns, pathologies, and paradoxes*. Faber and Faber.

Dealing with Difficult Conversations

The Way Conversations Go Sometimes Challenges Us

Contents

The explanations in this chapter are based on the following study brief: Lubienetzki, U. & Schüler-Lubienetzki, H. (2016). LASS UNS MITEINANDER SPRECHEN. GESPRÄCHSFÜH-RUNG. Study letter of the Fresenius University of Applied Sciences online plus GmbH. Idstein: Hochschule Fresenius online plus GmbH.

The world is real and not ideal. This realization inevitably leads to the conclusion that real conversations can deviate from the ideal course. Other people can work against a successful course of conversation for various reasons. We would like to recognise these in order to counter them with appropriate means.

4

⊜ **After Reading This Chapter in Depth, You Will Be Able to …**
━ Identify what **resistance** in communication is.
━ Resort to **intervention strategies** appropriate to the circumstances when resistance arises.
━ Recognise particular **manifestations of resistance**, such as manipulative behaviour or unobjective criticism, and explain how to deal with them.
━ Use **feedback** consciously in conversation.
━ Successfully **confront** your interlocutor, taking into account different approaches and strategies in the face of resistance.

4.1 Dealing with Resistance

When dealing with difficult conversational situations, such as resistance for example, it is important what attitude we adopt. If we perceive resistance exclusively as something negative, it is likely to trigger a defensive reaction in us. If we first deal with resistance in a non-judgmental way, it opens up the possibility of using it productively.

In the overview of meanings of the term *resistance*, the Cambridge University Press (n.d.-b) lists "a force that acts to stop the progress of something or make it slower" amongst others. The term has neither positive nor negative connotations. Based on this meaning, we can define resistance in communication with other people as follows:

┌─ **Definition** ───
│
│ **Resistance** is anything that prevents us achieving our goals when communicating with others.
│
└──

Gührs and Nowak refer to Freud (1972) and first describe everything as resistance that disturbs the continuation of the work. Subsequently, they go even further and define resistance as a creative attempt at a solution to eliminate a perceived deficit (Gührs & Nowak, 2014, p. 275).

The **manifestations of resistance** are numerous. It can be active or passive and expressed verbally or non-verbally. This results in the matrix in ◘ Fig. 4.1.

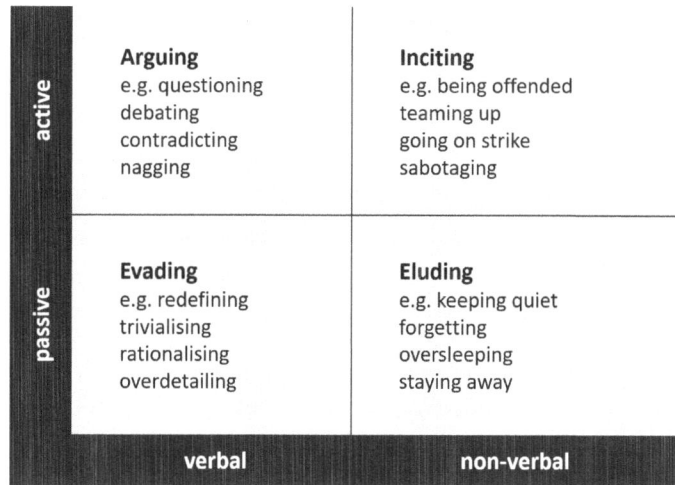

When people are resistant, this can be for many reasons. In relation to work with groups, according to Gührs and Nowak, resistance can be directed against "the topic", "the process", "the framework conditions" or "the leader" (Gührs & Nowak, 2014, p. 281). Following Gührs and Nowak (2014), we will now take a closer look at the motives for resistance in conversation.

Case Study

The trainees at Construction Machines Smith Ltd are very creative in refusing to engage in something they do not want for various reasons. Depending on the personality of the trainee, the resistance is expressed in different ways.

Let's take the trainee Ms Dissent as an example. She is very creative in contradicting her supervisor, Ms Baker. Instead of asking further questions on the matter, she systematically questions methods and approaches. Sometimes she even openly disagrees with "killer phrases" like "That's never worked before." or "It certainly won't work for us."

The trainee Mr Stall has a different strategy. He seems to give it some thought, but usually comes to the conclusion that it is not worth the effort or that something would have to be thought through in much more detail before a path could really be viable.

Sulking, crossing his arms and making deliberate mistakes are just some of the behaviours in Mr Abet's repertoire. Often, he joins forces with Mr Stall or Ms Dissent. In this case, he supports them in their verbal resistance by nodding vigorously or making other approving gestures.

Trainee Ms Skive is very hard to get hold of. Repeatedly she simply forgets the simplest matters. For example, she frequently doesn't show up for team meetings,

4

justifying her absence with the excuse, "I thought the meeting was cancelled." She also has the highest number of days off due to illness, and it is noticeable that these accumulate when unpleasant tasks are due.

4.2 Reasons for Resistance

If we perceive resistance in a conversation with another person, we might at first think that it is directed against us personally. In our experience, it is worthwhile to get to the bottom of the reasons for the resistance. Often the reasons lie somewhere else. But if we take the resistance personally, an inappropriate reaction on our part could miss its target and, moreover, have an escalating effect. Although the resistance could be directed against us, a **transference** of our interlocutor could be the reason for that. The resistance could also be directed against the topic of conversation, which, for example, triggers unpleasant feelings in our conversation partner. Finally, the reasons for the resistance could lie neither with us nor with the topic of conversation, but outside of it. Our interlocutor could be distracted by, for example, a private matter and therefore be reluctant to talk to us.

A goal-oriented **intervention**, i.e. a targeted measure or reaction with which we want to achieve a certain effect with our interlocutor, can only be successful if we know the motive behind the resistance well enough (Gührs & Nowak, 2014).

> **Definition**
>
> An **intervention** is a targeted measure intended to achieve a desired reaction (in our interlocutor) (cf. Wirtz, n.d.).

The second relevant dimension is the **impact** of resistance. As the negative impact of resistance on our personal goal achievement increases, our reaction also changes. In the extreme case, our interlocutor offers resistance, but this is almost meaningless for the achievement of our goal. Consequently, we do not necessarily have to react to the resistance (Gührs & Nowak, 2014).

If we create a matrix including the degree of acceptance of the motives and the degree of negative impact of the resistance, the **intervention strategies** shown in ◘ Fig. 4.2 emerge (Gührs & Nowak, 2014).

Following Gührs and Nowak (2014), the following **intervention strategies** are possible in conversations:
1. **Ignoring**: We perceive the resistance, but do not react to the resistance of our interlocutor.

> ▶ **Example: Distracted by What Is Happening Outside the Window**
>
> Our interlocutor is briefly distracted by a person they see outside the window. After a short pause, our interlocutor turns back to us and we resume the conversation without comment. ◀

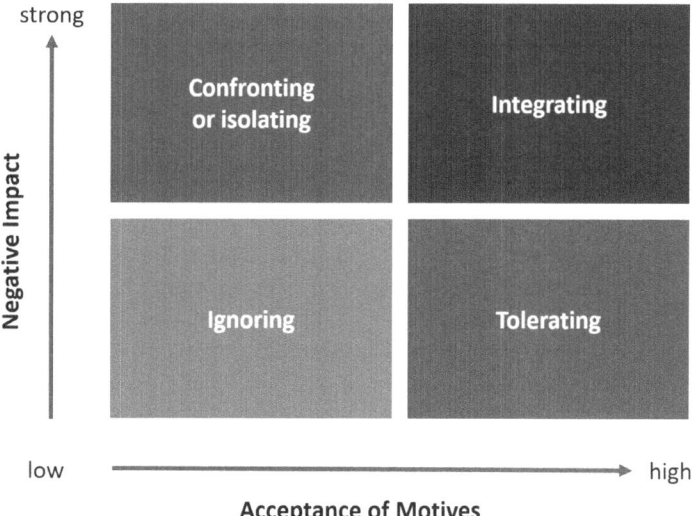

● **Fig. 4.2** Intervention strategies for managing resistance. (Source: own representation based on Gührs & Nowak, 2014, p. 282)

2. **Tolerating**: Similar to ignoring, we perceive the resistance, but in this case, we react to it. Our reaction should especially signal understanding, but without giving too much space to the motive of resistance.

❯ Note
Here the personal attitude is decisive: If we really accept the motive of resistance and not just grudgingly accept it, there is no conflict. If we gnash our teeth inwardly, we do not really accept the motive. We are more in the "ignore" field and better not comment on the behaviour. However, depending on how well developed our acting skills are, our inner gnashing of teeth will affect our behaviour and thus make our "feigned" tolerance untrustworthy.

▶ Example: Message on the Mobile Phone
Our conversation partner has informed us before our conversation that they might receive a message on their mobile phone during the course of the conversation. When the phone vibrates, we signal to them that they can accept the message and we briefly interrupt the conversation. ◀

3. **Confronting** (in groups it may be reasonable to isolate the person who is the cause of the resistance beforehand and address them during a break, for example): The resistance is greater and more disruptive to the flow of the conversation. We confront the interlocutor with their behaviour (▶ Sect. 4.4) with the aim of changing it.

4

▶ **Example: Parallel Conversation on the Mobile Phone**

Our interlocutor starts typing a message into their mobile phone in the middle of the conversation. After they have finished, they continue to look at the display. We inform our counterpart of our observation and that we feel disturbed by them using the mobile phone. We then ask them to put the mobile phone aside during the conversation. We leave them free to continue the conversation at another time if necessary. ◀

❯ **Important**

In this example, the situation and the relationship between the interlocutors is crucial. In the previous example, it could be a professional informational discussion between colleagues. However, if it is, for example, an appraisal interview in which an employee is using their mobile phone, the offer to continue the conversation later could be inappropriate in the situation.

4. **Integrating**: Also in this case, the resistance is so disruptive that the achievement of the goal is jeopardised. Such disruption must be dealt with. Since we have "understanding" for the motive, we signal our understanding and offer to integrate the topic of resistance into our conversation.

▶ **Example: Bad News During a Coaching Session**

In a coaching conversation on a professional topic, the client receives negative private news that is visibly bothering him. As a coach, we offer to work on the private issue first before continuing with the professional issue. ◀

❓ **? Reflection Task: Own Experience with Resistance**

Everyone goes into resistance at times, certainly you do too. Now analyse a situation in four steps in which you have resisted:
1. In which way did you resist? Please describe your behaviour at that time.
2. Now put yourself in the place of your counterpart who has perceived the resistance. Which goal pursued by this person did you thwart with your behaviour? What negative effect might have resulted from this?
3. What was your motive for resisting?
4. How did your counterpart react to your behaviour?

Now turn it around and analyse a situation where a person put up resistance to you:
1. What behaviour have you observed?
2. What was the negative impact on your target?
3. What guess do you have as to the motive for the behaviour?
4. How did you react at that time? Which intervention strategy would have been effective?

4.3 Special Forms of Resistance

We have already seen that the forms of resistance are extremely diverse. Often the resistance is rather harmless or even unconscious. In these cases, appropriate feedback is usually sufficient to move the interlocutor in the direction of a successful conversation.

In the following, we would like to discuss two manifestations of resistance – manipulative behaviour and unobjective criticism – which usually have a deliberately destructive goal. **Manipulative behaviour** aims at the realization of goals that deviate from the actual goal of the conversation. **Unobjective criticism** is usually directed against people and indirectly wants to prevent the actual goal of the conversation.

▬ **Manipulative behaviour**

Definition

Manipulation in a broad sense, according to Esch et al. (2016), is a form of influence in which (1) the influencer influences others for their own benefit, (2) chooses methods of influence that are not transparent to others, and (3) gives others the subjective feeling that they are free to choose.

Manipulative behaviour in conversation is a special form of resistance. According to the definition above, it aims at influencing the interlocutor in such a way that they accept – even against their will – the objective of the manipulator.

Manipulation has a wide variety of manifestations. In the book "How we talk to each other – the messages we send with our words and body language" we looked at the "games people play" according to Eric Berne (1966) and Lubienetzki and Schüler-Lubienetzki (2021). Let's take the "yes-but game" discussed there as an example. In the "yes-but game" the player tries to get confirmation of the unsolvability of their problem or situation. The underlying view of life tends to be negative ("I'm not okay."). Our interlocutor might try to get their life view confirmed via this game (Gührs & Nowak, 2014). Therefore, the manipulation is not necessarily directed against the actual goal of the conversation but focusses on the personal goal of our interlocutor. If we notice the manipulative intention and do not engage in the yes-but game, the negative effect is probably rather small. The situation is different if our interlocutor is acting with the intention of missing the actual goal of the conversation and pushing through their own goals. In this case the negative effect is clearly greater. In essence, such constellations of conversation are about gaining and exercising **power** over the interlocutor, which according to Weber (1976) is defined as follows:

Definition

Power means any chance to assert one's own will within a social relationship, even in the face of opposition (Weber, 1976, p. 28).

This view implies that manipulative behaviour in conversation is always unacceptable as a particular form of resistance. The intervention strategy for manipulative behaviour so depends exclusively on the negative impact of the manipulation. If it

4

is rather low, we can ignore it. If it is high, however, we must confront (▶ Sect. 4.4) and stop the manipulation attempt.

> **Important**
>
> In our book "Schwierige Menschen am Arbeitsplatz – Handlungsstrategien für den Umgang mit herausfordernden Persönlichkeiten am Arbeitsplatz" ("Difficult people at work – Action strategies for dealing with challenging personalities") (Schüler-Lubienetzki & Lubienetzki, 2015), which will be available in English soon, we have dealt in detail with the striving for power and manipulation. In ▶ Sect. 3.3 of the book, the toxic process is described, which at its core aims at manipulating other people. The objective of manipulation in this context is to realise egoistic personal motives (e.g. money, status, pleasure) that deviate from the company, regardless of any resulting harm.

Unobjective criticism

Another special form of resistance is unobjective or destructive criticism. We also count the so-called *killer phrases* among these. Unobjective criticism, as the name suggests, is not aimed at the factual content of the conversation, but at something else; it is usually directed against the interlocutor. It is clearly a form of resistance since this form of criticism always leads away from the actual goal of the conversation and impedes or even prevents the achievement of the goal. The negative impact is usually high, because this form of criticism is very deliberately designed to unsettle the interlocutor and distract from the actual topic or goal of the conversation.

Confronting the interlocutor with their unobjective criticism is therefore usually the only effective course of action. Of course, the unobjective criticism could also conceal an acceptable concern. However, since this is usually not obvious, an initial confrontation could lead to the need for integration.

4.4 Feedback and Confrontation: Another Person Learns Something About Themselves From Us

During the conversation, our interlocutor may wish to learn something from us about themselves and their behaviour. We can also say something about them and their behaviour without being asked if the occasion arises (e.g. in the case of resistance). Generally, in these cases we speak of giving **feedback** to someone else.

> **Definition**
>
> According to the Duden editors (n.d.), **feedback** is a reaction that indicates to someone that a certain behaviour, utterance, or the like is understood by the communication partner and has led to a certain behaviour or behavioural change.

Feedback can refer to the factual content of the conversation, the behaviour of our interlocutor, and the relationship between the interlocutors (cf. Gührs & Nowak,

2014; Schulz von Thun, 2013; Watzlawick et al., 1968). Moreover, it can contain a positive or negative appraisal or evaluation. With a positive appraisal, we pursue the goal of confirming or even reinforcing or strengthening our interlocutor. With negative appraisal, our desire is for the feedback to cause a change in the interlocutor; in this case, we speak of a **confrontation** (cf. Gührs & Nowak, 2014).

According to Schulz von Thun (2013), feedback as a message to the interlocutor has **four sides** (factual content, relationship, self-revelation, appeal) and is always heard with **four ears**.

> **▶ Example**
>
> We notice that our conversation partner repeatedly taps the table with their index finger during the conversation. We believe that they are unconsciously exhibiting this behaviour and call their attention to it, "May I give you some feedback?" – "Yes, of course." – "Since our conversation started, you have been tapping the table with your index finger."
>
> One response might be, "Yeah, right. That's such a quirk of mine and has nothing to do with you." Another might be, "Thanks for pointing that out, I hadn't noticed!" or, "Are we having a conversation or are you trying to point out my faults?" ◄

You see: Any of the reactions described would be plausible. In order to make sure that the feedback is understood correctly, you should give additional clarifying information about your own intention. The objective here is to ensure that the messages in the feedback are understood as they are meant (cf. Schulz von Thun, 2013).

In a conversation, the extent to which feedback can be coherently given depends on the relationship between the conversation partners as well as on the conversation situation. Ideally, the conversation partners have agreed in advance on the extent to which mutual feedback is desired (cf. Gührs & Nowak, 2014; Schulz von Thun, 2008).

When we address a problematic behaviour, i.e. give feedback with negative appraisal, we confront our interlocutor with it. In doing so, we pursue the goal of achieving a positive change in behaviour in the sense of the goal of the conversation.

■ Confrontation

> **Definition**
>
> According to the Cambridge University Press (n.d.-a) "to confront someone is to meet with a person with whom you disagree or whom you will accuse of something".

If the goal of the conversation is endangered due to the resistance of our interlocutor, we often only have the choice between confronting our interlocutor with their behaviour or breaking off the conversation. A termination of the conversation will certainly lead to our conversation goal not being achieved. Therefore, we should try to convince our interlocutor that their behaviour is burdening the course of the conversation by means of a goal-oriented intervention.

4

In this context, Gührs and Nowak (2014, p. 223) speak of the **art of confrontation**. By this they mean that confrontation always has something to do with pointing out something problematic in another person's behaviour. As a result, confrontation always bears a potential for conflict. In the language of transactional analysis, confrontation is a crossed transaction because it is usually unexpected for the interlocutor. Therefore, it triggers at least irritation, if not aggression, in them. The trick is therefore to use the confrontation to get our interlocutor to devote their energy to changing the problematic behaviour (Gührs & Nowak, 2014).

Following Gührs and Nowak, three aspects are important to achieve the goal of confrontation in conversation (2014):

1. **Preparing the interlocutor for the confrontation**
   If we are unexpectedly confronted with our problematic behaviour, we reflexively begin to justify ourselves and defend ourselves against the image that is conveyed to us about ourselves. Therefore, it makes sense to initiate the confrontation – for example, by giving an appropriate hint or by asking whether the interlocutor is interested in feedback. Of course, there may also be reasons (for example, in the case of a massive attempt at manipulation) to confront the interlocutor unexpectedly.

2. **Appreciative personal attitude**
   Confrontation should always refer to a clearly identifiable observation and not to a person as a whole. Therefore, the message we send out, due to our personal attitude, should show that we value the person and only criticise the problematic behaviour in question.

3. **Self-check**
   The constructivist view of communication by Watzlawick et al. (1968) or Schulz von Thun (2013) states that the messages received are to a large extent made by us and originate within us. We should definitely ask ourselves whether the behaviour we perceive as problematic actually endangers the goal of the conversation or whether we are reading something into the behaviour of our conversation partner from previous experiences that is not there at all.

As already mentioned, confrontation takes place on three levels, whereby these levels can also be understood in terms of escalation. Following Watzlawick et al. (1968), Schulz von Thun (2013) as well as Gührs and Nowak (2014), confrontation can start at the level of the factual content, at the level of the behaviour or at the level of the relationship:

1. **Factual content**
   At the level of factual content, the aim is to correct factual aspects. The interlocutor may have just made a mistake or confused the facts. Even if the factual content has been deliberately distorted or deliberately left unclear, it is worth confronting the factual content level. Only when we suspect there is a hidden agenda behind the problematic statements should we confront the behaviour on the next level.

2. **Behaviour**
   If the confrontation on the factual level repeatedly does not bear fruit or if we recognise a problematic pattern in the behaviour (e.g. multiple manipulative

attempts), we can confront our counterpart with corresponding behaviour. As long as the resistance is not rooted in the personal attitude of the interlocutor, this level of confrontation is sufficient. If the problematic behaviour does not stop or if the behaviour changes but the basic problematic pattern remains, the relationship level could be affected.

3. **Relationship**

Confrontation at the relationship level is the highest escalation level of confrontation. This is to uncover the pattern behind the problematic statements and behaviour. Confronting the interlocutor at this personal level should therefore really be the last stage of confrontation. Before doing so, it is essential to carefully check whether one's own perception might be incomplete (e.g. due to a "blind spot").

> **Important**

In our experience, people in professional contexts often tend to see the relationship level as problematic at a very early stage and confront it accordingly at an early stage ("Colleague XYZ can't stand me and puts obstacles in my way wherever possible"). This behaviour often manifests itself when resistance is seen as a personal attack or personal affront. Please keep in mind that there are many reasons for resistance in professional contexts (for example, a common reason is a person's personal overload with a task) and only in a few cases does the resistance primarily target the person or the relationship.

Case Study

John Smith happens to witness Mr Wilson reprimanding a trainee for misconduct. Mr Wilson stands in front of the trainee finger-pointing with his raised index finger, his face red and distorted with anger. His voice is clearly raised and John Smith hears the following: "Who do you think you are? You're hardly at a stage in your career to question someone as experienced as me! If I ask you to fetch me a coffee, then do it and don't argue with me about what you think your tasks are and what they are not. Now get out of my sight!" The trainee turns around and leaves. Mr Wilson watches him leave the room, shaking his head.

John Smith is very concerned about the incident. It is important to him that every employee in his company is treated with the same respect. He has heard several times and also experienced himself that Mr Wilson treats the trainees in this way. So he decides to confront Mr Wilson about his behaviour. He wonders how he could go about this.

Let's think about this together. Afterwards we will apply the options from the preceding case study.

We have already learned about one way of confronting a person. The **process of nonviolent communication** according to Rosenberg (2005) is suitable for confront-

4

ing a person in a very appreciative manner. The four components of nonviolent communication are:
1. Observations (no evaluations!)
2. Own feelings during observation
3. Own needs behind the feelings
4. My request to the interlocutor

Case Study

"Mr Wilson, I witnessed your conversation with the trainee earlier and would like to give you feedback on it. I heard your loud voice, your face was red. Among other things, you said to the trainee that he's hardly at a stage in his career to question someone as experienced as you and that he should not discuss with you whether getting coffee was his job or not. When I heard that, I was disappointed and alarmed. The reason for this is that I expect an appreciative attitude to be shown to all employees in our company. I did not perceive this in your behaviour. Therefore, I'm asking you to reconsider your attitude and to behave appreciatively towards the trainees in the future."

Gührs and Nowak (2014) propose **a three-step strategy** ("3-W-Strategie") (p. 237) for addressing problems:
1. My perception
2. The effect on me or on the conversation
3. My wish

Case Study

"Mr Wilson, you spoke very loudly with an apprentice earlier. Among other things, you said that he's hardly at a stage in his career to question someone as experienced as you and that he should not discuss with you whether fetching coffee is his job or not. What you said and your behaviour seem to me to be degrading to the apprentice. Therefore, I would like you to have an appreciative attitude towards trainees in the future."

As another variant, which probably has the most confrontational character, Gührs and Nowak (2014) propose **another version of the three-step strategy** ("3-F-Strategie") (p. 240):
1. Stating the facts
2. Consequences of the facts stated
3. Demands on the interlocutor

Case Study

"Mr Wilson, for the umpteenth time I have witnessed you talking loudly and with a red face to a trainee. Sentences such as You're hardly at a stage in your career to question someone as experienced as me!' and 'I don't want a discussion about whether fetching coffee is part of your job or not' were uttered. Such a derogatory attitude and your corresponding behaviour is unacceptable to me. Therefore, I urge you to base your behaviour toward trainees on appreciation and treat them accordingly in the future."

? Reflection Task: Application of Non-violent Confrontation and Three Step Strategies

In a previous reflection task you had already taken a closer look at your own situations in which you put up resistance. In which of the situations was an important goal not achievable for your counterpart? How would you have confronted yourself with your resistant behaviour in this situation? Formulate this along the four components of nonviolent communication as well as according to the three step strategies.

Summary in Key Terms

- As a rule, all participants in a conversation are interested in the conversation being successful. For various reasons, our conversation partner may feel the need to work against this goal. Since they thus stand in the way of our actual goal, they offer **resistance**.
  - Resistance is to be understood **value-free**, as it only indicates that our interlocutor wants to change something.
- The decisive factor is the **motive** behind the resistance, which does not always have to be obvious or be rooted in the acute situation.
- Depending on the **negative impact** of resistance on our personal goal achievement and our **understanding** of the motive of resistance, our **intervention strategy** is derived. Therefore, we can ...
  - ... ignore the resistance because it has no influence on the achievement of our goals.
  - ... tolerate the resistance by reacting with understanding without giving the motive much space.
  - ... confront the resistance by calling our counterpart on it, with the expectation that they will change their behaviour because we have no understanding of the motive.
  - ... integrate the resistance because we understand the motive.
- Manipulative behaviour and unobjective criticism both represent forms of resistance with a destructive goal.
  - **Manipulative behaviour** serves to achieve a goal that deviates from the actual goal of the conversation.

4

- Manipulation does not necessarily have to be unacceptable; if the negative impact is small, we can ignore it. If it has a decisive influence on the course of the conversation, we should confront our counterpart.
- **Unobjective criticism does** not concern the factual content of the conversation, but the interlocutor, and thus leads away from the actual goal of the conversation.
  - Confrontation is usually the only effective way to deal with unobjective criticism.
- **Feedback** is basically a way of giving our interviewee feedback on their behaviour.
  - Feedback can refer to the factual content of a message or the relationship level of the communicators or contain a positive or negative evaluation.
- If this feedback refers to a problematic behaviour, as in the case of resistance, and is linked to the expectation of a corresponding change in behaviour, it is referred to as a **confrontation.**
  - There are different approaches or strategies that should be considered in a confrontation depending on the situation and the relationship.
  - A confrontation can inadvertently lead to conflict if not handled prudently. To this end, three aspects should be considered during a confrontation:
    1. *Preparing* the interlocutor for the confrontation by giving a hint or asking whether the counterpart is interested in feedback
    2. Adopting an *appreciative* attitude by clearly referring to the problematic observable behaviour
    3. *Self-check* by questioning whether the behaviour we perceive as problematic actually affects the goal of the conversation.
  - Confrontation can start at three escalation levels, whereby these levels should be carefully addressed one after the other: the factual level, the behavioural level and the relationship level.
  - The *process of nonviolent communication* according to Rosenberg (2005) also offers a possibility for appreciative confrontation.
  - Alternatively, one can use the *three step strategies* according to Gührs and Nowak as a guide.

Literature

Berne, E. (1966). *Games people play. The psychology of human relationships*. Deutsch.

Cambridge University Press. (n.d.-a). Confront. In *Cambridge academic content dictionary*. Retrieved July 12, 2021, from https://dictionary.cambridge.org/dictionary/english/confront

Cambridge University Press. (n.d.-b). Resistance. In *Cambridge dictionary*. Retrieved July 12, 2021, from https://dictionary.cambridge.org/dictionary/english/resistance

Duden editors. (n.d.). Feedback. In *Duden online*. Retrieved July 12, 2021, from https://www.duden.de/node/45632/revision/45661

Esch, F.-R., Henning, A., & Schneider, W. (2016). Manipulation. In Springer Gabler Verlag (Ed.), *Gabler Wirtschaftslexikon*. Retrieved February 2, 2020, from http://wirtschaftslexikon.gabler.de/Archiv/56432/manipulationv4.html

Gührs, M., & Nowak, C. (2014). *Das konstruktive Gespräch. Ein Leitfaden für Beratung, Unterricht und Mitarbeiterführung mit Konzepten der Transaktionsanalyse* [The constructive conversation. A guide to coaching, teaching and personnel management involving concepts from transaction analysis] (7th ed.). Christa Limmer.

Lubienetzki, U., & Schüler-Lubienetzki, H. (2016). *Lass uns miteinander sprechen. Gesprächsführung* [Let's talk to each other. Conversation management] (Study letter of the Fresenius University of Applied Sciences online plus GmbH). Hochschule Fresenius online plus GmbH.

Lubienetzki, U., & Schüler-Lubienetzki, H. (2021). *Was wir uns wie sagen und zeigen. Psychologie der menschlichen Kommunikation* [How we talk to each other – The messages we send with our words and body language. Psychology of human communication]. Springer.

Schüler-Lubienetzki, H., & Lubienetzki, U. (2015). *Schwierige Menschen am Arbeitsplatz – Handlungsstrategien für den Umgang mit herausfordernden Persönlichkeiten* [Difficult people at work – Strategies for dealing with challenging personalities]. Springer.

Schulz von Thun, F. (2008). *Miteinander Reden 3 – Das "innere team" und situationsgerechte Kommunikation* [Talking to one another 3 – The "inner team" and situational communication] (17th ed.). Rowohlt.

Schulz von Thun, F. (2013). *Miteinander Reden 1 – Störungen und Klärungen* [Talking to one another 1 – Disturbances and clarifications] (50th ed.). Rowohlt.

Watzlawick, P., Beavin, J. H., & Jackson, D. D. (1968). *Pragmatics of human communication. A study of interactional patterns, pathologies, and paradoxes.* Faber and Faber.

Weber, M. (1976). *Wirtschaft und Gesellschaft: Grundriss der verstehenden Soziologie* [Economy and society: Outline of understanding sociology] (5th ed.). Mohr.

Wirtz, M. A. (n.d.). Intervention. In *DORSCH – Lexikon der Psychologie*. Retrieved July 21, 2020, from https://portal.hogrefe.com/dorsch/intervention/

Overall Summary in Key Terms

The explanations in this chapter are based on the following study brief: Lubienetzki, U. & Schüler-Lubienetzki, H. (2016). LASS UNS MITEINANDER SPRECHEN. GESPRÄCHSFÜH-RUNG. Study letter of the Fresenius University of Applied Sciences online plus GmbH. Idstein: Hochschule Fresenius online plus GmbH.

- **Conversation** is considered the most important form of human communication between two or more people.
- Communication in conversation is based on **verbal** and **non-verbal** expressions or what is **said** and the **behaviour** of the conversation partners.
- The participants perceive each other with all their senses and translate what they perceive into different messages.
  - The **perceived messages**, and thus also the chances of success of the conversation, are therefore largely dependent on the behaviour of the counterpart and their personal attitude.
- An individual's **personal attitude**, or mindset, can be viewed and influenced in a variety of ways.
  - Depending on how the personal attitudes of the parties involved in the conversation are pronounced and harmonise with each other, the chances of a successful conversation are higher or lower.
  - Someone's personal attitude is shaped, among other things, by ...
    - ... whether their **understanding of** the **relationship** with the respective interlocutor is based on *symmetry* (i.e. equality) or *complementarity* (i.e. inequality).
    - ... what the individual's **outlook on life** is in terms of acceptance and appreciation of self and others.
    - ... how an individual's **personality** is developed and whether it harmonises with the other person in terms of communication.
      An individual's personality can, for example, be classified according to the *Riemann-Thomann model*, according to which each person with their respective needs can be located in a coordinate system with the axes space (and the poles closeness and distance) and time (with the poles constancy and change).
  - An individual's personal attitude is reflected in their **verbal** and **non-verbal** communication.
    - If someone's personal attitude is inconsistent, this has a negative effect on the chances of a successful conversation, whereas a personal attitude that is conducive to conversation increases the chances of success of a conversation.
    - The personal attitude of a person is reflected, among other things, in congruent or incongruent communication. If the **digital** and **analogic modality**, i.e. the factual content of what is said and the behaviour displayed by a person, are not compatible with each other, the communication is **incongruent**. In these circumstances, the other person must decide how to interpret the perceived signals and which perceived message to respond to. Thus, the likelihood of a **communication breakdown** is very high.
- In addition to personal attitude, other factors play a role in successful **conversation**. These include, among other things, adequate preparation for the discussion as well as procedures that promote conversation during the dialogue.

— In order to **prepare** for a conversation situation in a **structured way**, it is a good idea to briefly analyse the following four points before or at the beginning of the talk:
  1. The background of the conversation
  2. The expected thematic structure
  3. The interpersonal structure
  4. The objective of the conversation.
— During the conversation, it is useful to be guided by the **operating principles of values-based conversation**, which means …
  1. Establish contact with the interlocutor
  2. To achieve clarity about one's own personal attitude
  3. To bring the personal attitude in line with the content and aim of the conversation
  4. To behave authentically ("genuinely")
  5. Listening actively (and really understanding the other person)
  6. Conduct the conversation in mutual harmony (with feedback).
— In every conversation it is advisable to communicate in a way that is **appropriate to the situation**. For this, the personal attitude and the conversation situation should be consistent.
    — If one becomes aware that one's personal attitude is not clear, the constellation of the **Inner Team** according to Schulz von Thun offers an opportunity to take a closer look at the individual aspects that shape one's own attitude in a particular situation.
— In principle, and in all conversations, we should **actively listen to** our conversation partners. It is helpful to ask questions and to communicate the background transparently, as well as to paraphrase what the other person has said in order to make sure that we understood them correctly.
— During the conversation, the targeted use of certain **questioning techniques** can be useful. An exemplary selection of question types are the information question, the alternative/decision question, the counterquestion, the motivating question, the shock/attack/provocation question, the solution-oriented question or also questions with manipulative intent, such as suggestive questions, rhetorical or indirect questions.
— The **concept of nonviolent communication** can also be used as a guide during a conversation in order to deal with the other person empathetically and thus promote the conversation. To do this, we should …
  1. Observe the other person and perceive without judgement
  2. Explore and express our own feelings
  3. Reveal the needs behind our feelings
  4. Formulate a positive request, the fulfillment of which will increase the quality of life of both conversation partners.
— When something in our communication prevents us from achieving our goal, it is usually **resistance** on the part of our interlocutor. Resistance can come in various forms and can be evaluated differently.
    — Crucial to the intervention strategy in the face of resistance are …

5

- — ... on the one hand, our counterpart's **motives** for resistance, which are not always obvious to us or based on the concrete situation or the participants in the conversation.
- — ... on the other hand, the negative **impact** of resistance on achieving our goal in the conversation.
- — Thus, four basic **intervention strategies** emerge:
    - — **Ignore** the resistance as it has little or no negative effect on our goal achievement and is irrelevant to the conversation.
    - — **Tolerating** resistance by showing genuine understanding for our counterpart without giving too much space to the motive of resistance.
    - — **Confronting** our counterpart's resistance, as it has a negative impact on our goal achievement, we do not accept it and expect our counterpart to change their behaviour.
    - — **Integrate** the resistance as we have understanding of our counterpart's motive.
- — In the case of particular **forms of resistance** such as manipulative behaviour or unobjective criticism, the number of effective intervention strategies is reduced.
    - — **Manipulative behaviour** that pursues goals which deviate from the actual goal of the conversation can be countered either with ignorance or with confrontation, depending on how great the negative impact of the resistance is.
    - — **Unobjective criticism** does not concern the factual content of the conversation, but rather the interlocutor and leads away from the actual goal of the conversation. It is usually best dealt with by direct confrontation.
- — Confrontation is a form of **feedback**. Feedback in general can contain a positive or negative evaluation, whereby the reaction of the person receiving the feedback depends on whether the feedback is compatible with the situation and the relationship of the parties involved in the conversation.
    - — Confrontation is feedback in the form of negative appraisal, coupled with the expectation of behaviour change.
    - — One can virtually speak of the "art of confrontation" when it achieves its goal, since this form of feedback is often **conflictual**. The goal of confrontation is that the feedback recipient spends their energy on a change of behaviour, not on countermeasures such as justifications, defiant or offended reactions.
- — For a **goal-oriented confrontation,** it is advisable to consider three aspects in advance:
    1. **Prepare** the interlocutor for the confrontation, for example by giving a hint or asking whether the counterpart is interested in feedback.
    2. Adopt an **appreciative** personal attitude, and always relate negative feedback to clearly identifiable observations in the here and now, not to the person as a whole.
    3. **Ask yourself** whether the behaviour perceived as problematic actually affects the goal of the conversation.
- — Confrontation can start at three **levels**, which should be examined in turn: the factual level, the behavioural level and the relational level.

—   The following approaches offer further guidance for successful confrontation:
    —   The already familiar **process of nonviolent communication**
    —   Provide feedback using the **three-step strategy**, communicating the following points:
        1. My perception
        2. The effect on me or the conversation
        3. My wish
    —   Alternatively, another **three-step strategy**:
        1. State the facts
        2. Name the consequences of the facts stated
        3. Make a demand on the interlocutor

Supplementary Information

© Springer-Verlag GmbH Germany, part of Springer Nature 2022
U. Lubienetzki, H. Schüler-Lubienetzki, *Let's Talk with Each Other!*,
https://doi.org/10.1007/978-3-662-64308-2

Glossary

Actualization tendency - The actualizing tendency describes a person's striving for the "development toward differentiation of organs and of functions, expansion in terms of growth, expansion of effectiveness through the use of tools, expansion and enhancement through reproduction" (Rogers, 1959, p. 196).

Attitude (synonymous with personal attitude) - Triandis (1971) states that "an attitude is an idea charged with emotion which predisposes a class of actions to a particular class of social situations." (p. 4)

Closed question - Closed questions specify the answer options (e.g. yes or no). This also includes questions that specify alternatives (adapted from Gührs & Nowak, 2014; Friedrichs & Schwinges, 2015).

Confrontation - According to the Cambridge University Press (n.d.) "to confront someone is to meet with a person with whom you disagree or whom you will accuse of something".

Feedback - According to the Duden editors (n.d.), feedback is a reaction that indicates to someone that a certain behaviour, utterance, or the like is understood by the communication partner and has led to a certain behaviour or behavioural change.

Intervention - An intervention is a targeted measure intended to achieve a desired reaction (in our interlocutor) (cf. Wirtz, n.d.).

Manipulation - According to Esch, Henning, and Schneider (2016), manipulation in a broad sense is a form of influence in which (1) the influencer influences others for his or her own benefit, (2) chooses methods of influence that are not transparent to others, and (3) gives others the subjective feeling that they are free to choose.

Open question - A question is open if it does not contain any restrictive specifications, such as answer options (adapted from Gührs & Nowak, 2014; Friedrichs & Schwinges, 2015).

Personality - According to the American Psychological Association (n.d.), personality is "the enduring configuration of characteristics and behavior that comprises an individual's unique adjustment to life, including major traits, interests, drives, values, self-concept, abilities, and emotional patterns."

Power - Power means any chance to assert one's own will within a social relationship, even in the face of opposition (Weber, 1976, p. 28).

Resistance - Resistance is anything that prevents us from achieving our goals when communicating with others.

Transference - According to Teuber (2016), transference is a central concept in psychoanalytic theory and practice which means that intense unconscious feelings, desires, sensations, or patterns of behavior from important past relationships are actualized in present relationships.

Index